ELK TACTICS

Advanced strategy for hunting and calling elk,
from the authors of *Elk Talk* and *The Elk Hunter*

By Don Laubach and Mark Henckel

Photos by Jim Hamilton
Illustrations by John Potter

Copyright © 1998 by Don Laubach and Mark Henckel

All rights reserved, including the right to reproduce
this book or any part thereof, in any form,
except for the inclusion of brief quotations in a review.

7 8 9 0 MG 20 19 18 17

Library of Congress Catalog Card Number 98-66697

ISBN 978-1-60639-007-8

(Previous ISBN 1-56044-682-X)

Published by:
Don Laubach
Box 85
Gardiner, MT 59030

Produced by Gans, Newby & Klein, Helena and San Francisco

Illustrations by John Potter
Cover and text photos by Jim Hamilton

Manufactured in the United States of America

ELK TACTICS

Dedication

This book is dedicated to all hunters who have hiked the trails of elk country before us, with grateful thanks that they shared what they learned, so that we could be better elk hunters today.

ACKNOWLEDGMENTS

All of us are products of those who come before us—the fathers, mothers, uncles, aunts, brothers, sisters, and others—who have shaped our lives. For these people, we give thanks. Without them, we'd never be who we are.

In our hunting lives, the same is true. We owe a debt of thanks to all the hunting partners who learned skills along with us, too often by trial and error or by bumbling and stumbling. We owe a debt to the wildlife biologists who put their considerable skills to use in filling elk country with huntable populations of elk. We owe a debt to the elk themselves, for being so wonderful and for filling so many happy days.

And if you've ever done a book, you know that perhaps the biggest debts are the ones you owe to your family. For all the hours that wives were neglected, children were ignored, and even the family pets were slighted, we offer our deepest apologies and our sincerest thanks.

TABLE OF CONTENTS

Foreword ix
    A Trilogy? From Us? ix

Introduction xi
    Deliver Me from Experts xi

Chapter One 1
    The New Elk 1
    Elk Are the Same 3
    Elk Are Different 11
    What Are the Elk Saying? 18

Chapter Two 27
    Where to Hunt 27
    Dissecting a Mountain 29
    Elk Travel Plans 40
    Reading Sign 52

Chapter Three 71
    When to Hunt 71
    Elk at Dawn 73
    The Neglected Noon Hunt 84
    The Evening Hunt 95

Chapter Four 107
    How to Hunt 107
    Planning a Hunt 108
    The Setup 120
    Dealing with Problem Elk 132

Chapter Five 143
   How to Make Elk Talk 143
   Elk Sounds 145
   Seen and Unseen Elk 158
   Call a Little, Call a Lot 172

Chapter Six 181
   Gearing Up 181
   Rifles and Bows 183
   Clothing and Camo 189
   Decoys 196
   Technology 201

Chapter Seven 207
   Troubleshooting 207

Epilogue 221
   Down the Trail 221

FOREWORD

A Trilogy? From Us?

Elk Talk
The Elk Hunter
Elk Tactics

Who would have thought we'd end up writing three books on elk hunting? In all truth, we never figured we'd write even one book. Honest.

Hunting is one of those really personal things. You have your very own hunting spot. You go there with only your family and your closest friends. You spend some of the finest moments of your life hunting. And even if there are other people out there with you in the same area, you still hold the experiences you come home with so near and dear to your heart that it's hard to imagine you'd ever share them.

In truth, we still feel that way. Elk, and the country elk live in, are special. Elk are the grandest big game animal of them all, and one of the greatest challenges a hunter can face. Elk country is simply spectacular, whether you're in Colorado, Arizona, Wyoming, Idaho, Utah, Oregon, British Columbia, Alberta, or Montana, where we live. We wouldn't trade our elk hunting experiences over the years for anything. And the skills we've gathered at elk hunting over the years are something we're justifiably proud of.

But we'd be lying to you if we told you that we knew all there is to know about elk hunting. All elk hunters are the product of the elk hunters who preceded them. We didn't invent the .30-06 or the compound bow. We weren't the first ones who bugled for elk. We haven't done studies on elk habitat use or antler development. Our hunting skills are a measure, in large part, of the older hunters we tagged along with in our youth, our partners of today, and other hunters we've learned about or read about over the years.

Now, it's time for us to share our knowledge, giving freely in that same spirit, so that others can enjoy hunting elk and calling elk the same way we do.

Those were the feelings that spawned *Elk Talk*. When we learned a little more and felt we had more to share, *The Elk Hunter* came about. Look at *Elk Tactics* as the next installment—perhaps the last, perhaps not—to further explain tactics from the first two books and talk about new tactics that have developed since then. Will there be a fourth book? That all depends on what new things we learn about elk and elk hunting in the years to come.

That's our investment in the future of elk, elk calling, and elk hunting. What's yours? It's our fondest wish that you come away from this book with a feeling of excitement about tactics you can try on elk and new ways to look at elk country. We hope that you share that knowledge with others, so that all of us can learn to be better hunters. We hope that your experiences in elk country will enrich your life in all the years to come.

>Don Laubach
>Gardiner, Montana

>Mark Henckel
>Park City, Montana

INTRODUCTION

Deliver Me from Experts

When I was a young elk hunter, I looked to the experts. I imitated the experts. I worshipped the experts. I wanted so badly to be an expert myself. That meant anyone, whether they had a byline in an outdoor magazine, put on a hunting seminar at a sports show, puffed and strutted at elk-calling competitions, or gave endorsements to gun or cartridge companies, was a hunting hero to me. These were the experts. These were the people who knew everything. These were the people I wanted to be. And anybody who wasn't an expert elk hunter really wasn't worth my time.

Maybe it's because I'm a lot older now. Maybe it's because I'm getting ornery in my old age. Maybe it's because I've seen and heard too many of these so-called experts over the years who weren't really experts. All I know is that the term "expert" has been so badly abused and so loosely passed around that the only emotions it elicits from me these days range from mild distrust to downright blatant contempt.

Lord, deliver us from these experts.

Consider the following statements of outdoor wisdom I've heard from the experts over the years (all of which have been positively debunked by others):

"Coyotes do not prey on mule deer. And if they do take a few, it's only the young fawns, just after they're born. They never take adults." (Coyotes can and do take adult mule deer, especially in years when other prey is scarce. Coyotes will hunt in pairs and packs for them, too. Coyotes will have their best success on the weak, the sick, the very old, and the very young, but they'll take healthy adults, too. And if they've got deep snow or ice to help them, coyotes can survive on a diet of mule deer.)

"If you fall in a river in waders, the weight of the water in the waders will pull you down. You can't swim in waders, and you'll drown." (Seriously, folks, when you fall in and your waders are under water, how can water inside the waders weigh more than water outside of them? Swimming in waders may be cumbersome and trying to climb out of a river with full waders may be tough, but when you're submerged or paddling around, the water inside and outside of your waders weighs the same. But panic that you might drown could kill you.)

"You can't call in antelope. You can't call in white-tailed deer. You can't call in mule deer. They just don't respond to calls." (Yes, they do. Yes, you can. All of these animals make sounds to each other, many of which are too soft for most of us to hear. In groups, and singly, these animals do make noises that others of their species respond to. These sounds can be imitated by us, even if we don't know exactly what we're saying in animal language. And every one of these animal species—bucks and does—has been called in and taken by hunters.)

"To call in a bull elk, you've got to sound like a bull elk. And even then, you can only call them in at the peak of the rut." (This was a common statement before the cow call became popular. Since then, hunters have found out that they can use a cow call to pull in bulls and cows and calves year-round.)

"The world is flat." (That guy has obviously never huffed and puffed up a mountain trail in elk country.)

You get the idea. And it should tell you about the experts.

Now, before we paint this expert situation with too broad a brush, let me state, too, that there are good and legitimate outdoor writers out there. There are some very good hunters among the callers at competitions. And some of those guys giving product endorsements are good hunters, too. But to tag anyone with the label of expert and expect them to be all-knowing and all-good and all-honest is going too far.

After watching elk hunting change over the years, I'm convinced that the truth of the matter is that no one is really an expert, and often people with some awfully shaky or outdated knowledge are the ones who try the hardest to sell themselves as being experts. Even worse, they sometimes hold themselves up on high as experts in the hopes that young and inexperienced hunters will worship and adore them. Those are the ones that really gall me. No elk hunter is a god, even with a little g, much less with a big one.

As for me, I take a little different view of elk, elk hunting, and elk hunters. I like to think of all elk hunters—you and me and everybody else—as simply being students of the elk-hunting game. Some students may be more advanced than others. Some students may know a little less. Others may know a little more. Some are working harder to learn. Some aren't working too hard at all. And still others are buying their knowledge from outfitters and guides each season, without ever caring to learn much about it themselves, and passing it off as knowledge of their own. But the bottom line is that all elk hunters have some level of knowledge. All have something to share. All have the ability to add to the wealth of insight and skills that could make you and me better hunters. But nobody, and I mean nobody, knows it all. Nobody is an expert.

Realizing that all of us are students of the game, another oddity I've observed over the years is that the most knowledgeable hunters I've ever met—the ones who came the closest to really being experts—have also been the hunters who were the most humble about their knowledge. When you talked to them, they passed on their knowledge almost as an afterthought. When you hunted with them, they taught more by example than by proclamation. And if you ever accused them of being experts, they'd have laughed in your face. It was almost as if they realized that the more they learned about elk, the more questions came to their minds. The more variables they factored into situations, the more they realized the answers weren't so easy. And, in the end, it seemed they came to an understanding with themselves that they still had so much to learn.

If there's a theme or a message you should take to heart from reading this book, it's that all of us are still learning about elk and elk hunting. When we find our first success, or add on to past successes, we can't afford to stop there. We have to keep experimenting. We have to keep trying. We have to keep observing. We have to keep learning.

As so many experts should have learned from their mistakes in the past, there aren't too many absolutes in this world. Things we took for granted yesterday might not hold true today. Notions about elk and ideas on elk-hunting tactics are still open for discussion, for trial and error, and for new ideas. That's how we all grow.

Suffice it to say that this book is not being written by experts—just students of the game who are comfortable in that role. We hope to pass on some of the knowledge we've gained with our hunting partners in elk country. This is being done not in the spirit of setting ourselves up on any lofty pedestal—perish the thought—but in the hope that you, too, as a fellow student, will come away with new knowledge and can add your experiences to the wealth of knowledge on elk. We'll tell you up front, we don't have all the answers. We don't even know all the questions yet. But we've spent a lot of time out there studying and trying to learn. We've picked up a few tips and tactics along the way, too, that should interest you if you're an elk hunter. And between you and me, in the pages ahead, we should all have some fun as we learn, and we share, and we explore, the wonderful world of elk and elk hunting today.

CHAPTER ONE

The New Elk

Elk hunting is all about challenges. There is the challenge of the elk themselves. There is the challenge of the terrain they live in. There are the personal challenges that you put on yourself to shoot a trophy bull, a big bull, any bull, or any elk. Put all these challenges together, and you've got a sport that's far from easy, that stirs excitement in your soul, and that brings a thrill to your psyche and a glow of satisfaction to your heart, especially when everything comes together and you achieve success in elk country.

That thrill and the satisfaction of elk hunting are things that haven't changed over time, even for hunters like me who have taken many more elk than I have fingers and toes and have the gray hair to prove my many years in the field. What has changed, however, is the way we go about elk hunting today and many of the challenges we face.

With each passing year, hunters change. They have more and better tools at their disposal to conquer the challenges of the elk themselves and the country they live in. Those tools include better rifles, optics, and ammunition. They include better clothing and camping gear. They include more versatile four-wheel-drive vehicles. They include calls and camouflage and decoys. They include time in the field that many never used to have.

The elk hunter himself has evolved—and evolved a lot. In many ways, it's easier to be an elk hunter now than it was in the old days. Transportation is certainly better, whether you live in the heart of elk country or thousands of miles away. There are more elk in more places than we've ever had before. Elk herds are better managed. Their habitat is more closely watched. They're trapped and transplanted, and herds can now be found almost from coast to coast. As a result, interest in elk is higher than it has ever been before in our lifetimes. And it's possible today for more people to be elk hunters, almost no matter where they live. It's easier for those elk hunters to gain a wide range of information about elk hunting and to be more knowledgeable hunters, whether it's from reading books like this one, watching videotapes about elk, attending seminars put on by a wise old hunter, or simply accessing the Internet.

But with this growth of hunter numbers and of better-informed hunters has come a change in the elk, too. Although they may be the same critters physiologically that they've always been, they've been forced to adapt mentally to the change in the game. In the past, when a six-point bull elk had only one or two hunters invade his territory through the course of a season, he didn't have to be too wise in the ways of man to survive. Now, a six-point bull might face dozens of hunters over the course of the season, and if his wits aren't sharp, he might not live to see the season end.

This hunting pressure, which has forced elk to be smarter than they were in the old days, has forced elk hunters to be smarter, too. In short, hunters have to be prepared not just for the elk, but for the other hunters. They have to use calls more wisely. They have to read sign more wisely. They have to adapt to both the elk and to the other hunters.

In some ways, we are all hunting the same old elk. In other ways, there's a whole new breed of animal out there being hunted in a whole new way. It's the wise hunter—and most often the successful one—who prepares himself to meet the challenge of elk hunting both by knowing the ways of the same old elk and by adapting to the new ways of hunting them.

Elk Are the Same

The high country around Gardiner, Montana, is comfortable to me. For almost thirty years, I've hiked the valleys here. I've glassed the high basins. I've traversed the alpine plateaus. In summer, I've cast my fishing line into its rushing streams and its clear blue mountain lakes. Each fall, I've grabbed my bow or slung my rifle and hunted deer and elk and grouse and bighorn sheep and moose and bears. In winter and spring, I've hiked, skied, or ridden by snowmobile far and wide.

All in all, this area just north of Yellowstone National Park is a great place to call home, surrounded by beautiful real estate, blessed with many thousands of acres of public land, hundreds of miles of trails, pristine forests, bountiful grass,

Elk today are the same as those our forefathers hunted, and their physical needs are the same, too.

Chapter One

ELK TACTICS

blankets of wildflowers, creeks, streams, and rivers, and enough bird and animal life to keep a song in your ears and a smile in your heart just about every minute you spend outdoors here. For a man of the mountains like me, this country is everything you could look for in life. And I've spent the better part of my lifetime here for just that reason.

But as much as my kids look at me as an old man of the mountains and a permanent fixture in this part of the country, I know better. I'm a newcomer and a short-timer here. I always will be. And so will you be in your chosen part of elk country.

The realization of that fact came early on in my hunting career. I was walking a well-traveled game trail, one that I'd traveled often before, cut deep into the side of a mountain when it dawned on me. I stopped. I took a few steps off to the side of the trail. I walked a ways. And then I looked back. My footprints on that mountainside were invisible on the dry ground. Had it been wet ground, I might have seen a little more sign of my passage, but not much. If that was the case, how many elk steps, deer steps, animal steps had it taken to cut that well-traveled game trail I'd been walking? In places, that trail was a foot deep. In places, it was several feet wide. That trail had been traveled for many centuries, at least. It had been a daily route of travel for countless generations of elk and other wild game. And little by little, step by step, they had cut an incredible path on that mountainside that I used only infrequently. Even in my whole lifetime of hiking that trail, I'd make hardly a dent in the earth. The animals had cut a veritable highway.

The little lesson of that elk path made me realize that, in effect, just about all the elk we're hunting are old-timers and long-timers to the country in which they live. They've been doing their thing here and in other parts of elk country for generations. There are things in that country that sustained the elk's ancestors and continue to sustain the existing generation of elk. That the elk still use these trails, and are thriving by using them, must mean that elk are the same creatures they've always been. That's only logical.

Cow elk look for key security areas when it comes time to drop their calves in spring.

So, if you look at the physical needs of elk, we really are hunting the same critters that our forefathers hunted. Elk need grass and other things to eat on a daily basis, just as they always have. They need water to drink. They need security cover to bed in. They need lush summer range in the warm season and generally lower-elevation winter range to survive the winter. They need migration paths in between, too. Bull elk still grow a new set of antlers each year. They breed in the weeks of September and early October each year. Bulls still use wallows. They still rub their antlers. There are still herd bulls, satellite bulls, and a bunch of confused spikes, their lives all surrounding those of the harems of cows and calves. It's all still the same as it always was.

That being the case, it should be possible to successfully hunt elk in the same way our forefathers hunted them because, obviously, the elk are the same.

Hunters who live by this creed are on the right track. No matter what tactics you employ in your elk hunting, you have to remember the basic needs of elk. You have to know about their basic daily needs. You have to know about their

Chapter One

ELK TACTICS

lifestyle. You have to know these things because they form the basis of where you look for elk in the first place.

The best elk caller in the world isn't going to call in elk if there aren't any elk out there to be called.

One of the best parts about living in Gardiner, in the heart of good elk country, is the ability to be around elk and observe them, not just during a week or two of hunting season, but all through the year.

Taking advantage of that opportunity, one of the things I've been able to do since our last book, *The Elk Hunter*, is to keep track of a group of elk for pretty much an entire year. That chance firmed up some of my suspicions about elk, among them the fact that basic needs are the driving force behind elk behavior and influence their distribution totally until some outside factor forces them to change.

There were around twenty-two head of cows that comprised the group and just six calves with them that survived. For the most part, I usually stayed quite a ways away from them when I observed them. There were also three bulls that stayed close to these cows and calves and associated with the herd, but they often stayed lower on the mountain than the cow-calf group.

It was easy to figure out their summer pattern. It revolved around where the elk would feed and where they'd water. If you knew where that was in the area, it was pretty easy to keep track of them, just as long as the herd wasn't bothered. If somebody or something came into the area and spooked them, it was a week or so until they'd return to their home area again.

The group's activities were totally predictable, and they held in that home area, making the most of the food, water, and security it offered, until the week before archery season, during the latter part of August. With the coming of the rut, the group moved from their home. In fact, they moved away for a month and a half, which roughly coincides with the time just before, during, and just after the rut. They didn't return to their home range until clear into October.

During the time of that absence, these cows, calves, and

bulls were responding to another of their basic needs, the need to reproduce and continue their species. Based on my years of hunting elk in the rut with a bow and arrow, I was pretty sure where the group had moved. I didn't have the time to climb to the tops of the mountains and start looking on the north slopes and the places where they did the breeding, but I know that's where they went. It's where the elk always go during the breeding season.

When they returned to their home range, the basic pattern the elk had followed all summer long returned. The three bulls—one a six-point and the other two smaller brush bulls—would lie in the same general area during the day. The six-point usually lay by himself. The two brush bulls lay a little distance away from him. I never did find them when they were lying together. The big bull was always anywhere from fifteen to twenty yards away from the younger bulls.

When winter came, the elk moved down the drainage to lower elevations, mixing with other migratory herds that had come to that elevation for the same reason. But when spring arrived, my herd of elk moved back toward their home territory, once again drawn by the basic life factors that made it so appealing to begin with, the food, water, and security. Calves were dropped on a surprisingly steep hillside, covered with sparse timber and sagebrush. I would have figured they'd have calved out lower, but they were halfway up the mountain. Probably the reason was one of security. Farther up on the mountain, they weren't subject to as much harassment by human traffic. They were in a remote area where they could have the solitude they needed.

One of the things that observing these elk confirmed to me is that when you have elk native to a drainage, and if their basic needs are being met there, they'll stay in that drainage until something forces them to leave. In fall, if it wasn't for the rut and hunting pressure, my elk herd would never have left the area. But the bodily urges of the rut moved them early in the fall. Later, it was an influx of hunters that caused them to move away for a time. What this taught me was that if you pattern elk in a drainage and

Chapter One

ELK TACTICS

know where their food sources are, where the water is available, where their bedding areas are and all the paths in between, you can count on finding elk there if you know where they're likely to be in each of the seasons.

Understanding how hunters and human traffic can move elk is pretty easy. You watch hunters go into a drainage.

Elk communicate with each other in a variety of ways, both verbally and by touch.

You watch elk run out. You realize that human disturbance has altered the situation in an area and that one of the animals' basic needs—the need for security and to be left alone—is gone.

Persistent predators can also affect elk and move them out of an area. In my hunting area, the appearance of a new predator, the wolves that have been introduced into Yellowstone National Park, has already begun to change things. Those wolves, though introduced into the park, have grown in number quickly and have ranged far and wide beyond the park boundaries. Their tracks have become relatively common in the many places I wander. I'm sure they'll be even more common in more elk hunting areas in the future. But most interesting to me is that one of the places I found tracks, and the wolves that made them, was in the drainage where I followed those elk.

Although it's too early to assess many of the effects these wolves will have on the ecology of the region, it was the appearance of two wolves in that drainage last spring that provided me with a strong lesson about persistent predators and elk. Grass was just starting to green up and the cow elk hadn't calved out yet when I spotted the wolves. Groups of elk were still inhabiting the winter range. They were walking traditional paths up and down the drainage. And I was glassing the newly green mountain slopes for elk when I spotted the wolves.

What followed was quite a little drama. As elk herds moved up the slope, one wolf moved off and the other lay down under a tree, watching the elk come closer and closer. The first herd to arrive near the tree had roughly twenty head of elk in it, made up of cows and calves. As soon as the elk came close enough, the wolf darted out from its hiding spot and tried to grab one of them. With the rush, the elk herd dispersed, with members of a lower group all facing the wolf. One cow elk, which the wolf cut off from the herd, immediately ran to a tree and stood with its butt against the tree trunk. The wolf kept walking around the elk and the tree, and the elk kept going around and around, its butt firmly defended by the tree trunk. The other wolf

ELK TACTICS

stayed up on the hill and watched.

One of the yearling elk in the herd, which must not have been aware of what was going on and must have been the cow's calf from the previous year, came over to where the cow was. The wolf made a run at the yearling, and the cow left the tree and chased the wolf, as the yearling ran off.

The wolf finally gave up on that pair of elk and went back to its original post under the tree, waiting for another group of elk to come along from farther down the slope. When that group arrived, the wolf ran out again, and again tried to grab a meal. This group of elk all formed a half-circle and faced him. The wolf made some false charges against this defense, but the elk held their ground. After a short time, the wolf left the elk and took off on a dead run toward the first wolf.

It shouldn't come as a big surprise that the appearance of the wolves changed the pattern of the elk in the area in the weeks that followed. I have a hunch that, since it was the spring of the year and there were at least two wolves in there, they probably had a den somewhere nearby. Since the wolves' arrival, I haven't seen the elk there. Apparently, the wintering elk pulled out and the elk native to the drainage pulled out as well.

The persistent presence of a predator had altered the lifestyle of the native elk herd. One of the herd's basic needs wasn't being provided anymore—the need for security. With wolves taking up residency, especially in the spring when calves would be dropped, it was time for the elk herd to find a new home. Where that home is, I really don't know. With some hiking in the months ahead, perhaps I'll find them and recognize them. Perhaps I won't.

One of the more interesting things I'll have to watch for and learn about in the future is whether or not the elk will move back into the drainage if and when the wolves move out. In the many years I've hunted near Gardiner, that drainage has been a favorite of mine during the hunting season. I've known the elk there well. I know where the food, water, and security areas are located and all the paths in between. I've learned where the elk live and what they do in all seasons of the year. And, during the fall, I've always managed to get a bull in there whenever I wanted one. Will the wolves stay? Will the elk come back? Where will the elk move if they don't come back? Will traditional paths traveled for centuries by elk be untouched by the hoof prints of elk in the years ahead?

Understanding the basic needs of elk will carry a hunter a certain distance in his pursuit of elk. This is base knowledge that every elk hunter must have. But there are other factors at work in the elk-hunting equation. Elk hunting isn't the same as it always has been. And as a result, elk hunters are going to have to adjust.

Elk Are Different

Postgraduate elk. That's the way one hunting partner described them. These were elk that were so smart that they'd gone beyond elementary and secondary schooling from hunters. They'd graduated from dealing with college-level hunting tactics, too. They had advanced all the way to postgraduate studies in driving hunters nuts.

The elk being described were the ones found in the Missouri Breaks of north-central Montana. And they were only being pressured by bowhunters!

While rifle hunters in the Breaks are limited in number by special permits, the area was wide-open to bowhunters. And bowhunters by the hundreds had flocked into the area each September and early October. They had stalked, still-hunted, driven, tree-standed, and called the elk there to the point that every trick in the hunter handbook had been tried on the local herd. The elk there, hunters say, cannot only tell the brand name of the call being used by a hunter, but can tell whether it's the latest model or an older one. They say the elk even whisper among themselves, rating the hunters on a scale of 1 to 10 as to how good or bad they are. These are very, very, very smart elk.

Unfortunately, these elk are not alone. Whether you talk to hunters from Colorado, Wyoming, Idaho, Utah, Oregon,

Chapter One

■ *ELK TACTICS*

*With increasing hunting pressure,
elk have become almost totally nocturnal in some areas.*

or anywhere else in elk country, you'll hear the same thing. The elk they are hunting these days are not the same elk they hunted years ago. Elk are smarter now than they used to be. Or, at least, they're better adapted to foiling the best efforts of hunters—efforts, I might add, that were plenty good enough to bag bulls years ago.

This new breed of elk—these elk that are different—are elk that have learned to cope with the new wave of hunting pressure. They've learned tactics of their own to cope with hunters who are so adept at calling that they sound even better—to the human ear anyway—than elk themselves. These are pressured elk, and they're very, very tough.

If your hunting area is like this, you're not alone. Questions about how to hunt pressured elk come up at every seminar I've ever given. Questions about them come in the mail. Questions about them come from everywhere.

But before we get to some possible answers, let's look first at the problem and, in doing that, better understand the factors that are at work here.

Pressured elk are basically elk that have either seen somebody before you or see somebody while you're calling. These are elk that are too familiar with humans. They reveal this familiarity in a variety of ways.

We'll use the Missouri Breaks of Montana as just one example. In the river bottoms there—where tall old cottonwoods are mixed with impenetrable willow thickets—the elk have been hunted from tree stands so often that they have learned to look up. As a result, hunting from any reasonable height in the tree often results in elk that spot you long before you spot them. Successful hunters have had to climb higher and higher and—stop here for a nosebleed—higher yet.

The elk have learned to listen for telltale sounds of hunters, as well. One of those telltale sounds might be the slightly metallic sound of a willow rapping against the aluminum handle of a compound bow. It might be the corrugated step of a heavy-treaded boot sole rubbing over rock-hard mud. It might be the click of a plastic snap on a pack. It might be the rip of a Velcro closure being opened. It might be just about anything that isn't a natural sound. As far as calling those elk is concerned, the elk have learned to associate sounds coming from humans with the sounds of an elk call.

The first thing you'll notice about these pressured elk is that they become very silent. They may bugle and talk at night, but at any hour during daylight, you'll hear nary a sound. Another thing I've noticed is that their use of silence as a survival tactic goes beyond the animals not being vocal. The elk also use silence to test the patience of hunters—waiting them out until they almost invariably give themselves away by making some sort of noise.

The best example of that was a stalk I was trying to make on a bugling bull in one of those dense willow jungles that the river bottoms are so famous for. This bull had been bugling for at least an hour, moving slowly through a 100-yard-wide corridor of willows that paralleled the river on one side and an open, dry creek channel on the other.

I was trying to work that bull from the dry creek channel side, waiting for him to find a suitable place to cross that

Chapter One

■ ELK TACTICS

channel and move to bedding areas further inland. It was easy enough to keep track of the bull, even without the deep-throated bugles and grunts he was emitting every ten minutes or so. I could hear his antlers hitting the willows whenever he moved. I could hear the crunch of his big body moving through the tangles, too. Slowly, steadily, the elk

Elk will stand for long periods of time, not making a sound, waiting for a hunter to betray his presence.

was moving up the corridor, not all that far in from the dry channel.

I paralleled that bull for almost a half-hour, walking quietly in the sand and soft earth. When he stopped, I stopped. When he started crunching willows, I'd move along with him, carefully slipping through the scattered willows growing up in the channel. But after that half-hour, I made a mistake. One of the willows slipped from my hand and rapped against my bow handle. The sound didn't seem all that loud to me, but it was as if someone turned off a switch on that elk. The bugling ended right then and there. The animal never took another step. It became a battle of wills and a battle of patience.

I stood in the creek channel. The bull stood in the willows, probably not fifty yards away from me. We stood there. And we stood there. And we stood there. Five minutes passed. Then ten minutes. Then fifteen minutes. Then twenty.

I could see him in my mind's eye, standing there like a statue. I'm sure his ears were working hard, trying to listen for the slightest noise that was out of place. I'm sure his nose was hoping for some sort of breeze to carry my scent to him. I'm sure he was looking my way, hoping to see something through that wall of willows, something that would verify the source of that single errant noise.

After thirty minutes of waiting, the standoff was still going strong when another bowhunter came walking down the channel. That bowhunter made just enough noise that the elk's suspicions were confirmed with ease. When the noise got close—and then the bowhunter said softly, "Hi, how ya doing?"—the bull blew out of there, never to be seen again.

The bowhunter said he was surprised there was an elk so close. I never told him that I knew the bull was there. I just smiled. I said I was doing fine. And I tucked the experience away, wondering to myself how many times I'd been so close to elk that had stood there like statues, monitoring the noises I made, verifying to themselves that I was a hunter, and then sneaking away if they could, quietly letting me pass, or exploding out of the country like this bull had.

In the Missouri Breaks, and areas like it, the pressurized

Chapter One

ELK TACTICS

education of elk is extreme. There's plenty of road access. There are plenty of places for hunters and sightseers to get on a high point, glass the country, sound their calls, and in the process, educate every elk within earshot and sight-line. Of all pressurized elk scenarios, these are the worst. And places like them, with plenty of easy hunter access and plenty of hunter traffic, are found in virtually every elk state and province.

But it really doesn't take that much pressure to turn out an educated elk. Elk can be educated much more easily than that. In fact, all it takes is a hunter or two or three, if those hunters really work at it.

All an elk has to do is to hear an elk call, respond to it, and have a sour situation develop. An elk will remember it. If an elk comes in and spots a hunter instead of an elk, that elk's education has begun. If an elk comes in and smells a hunter instead of an elk, the experience adds to that education. Certainly, if an elk comes in and gets an arrow or a bullet sent in his direction, that's going to add to that elk's education.

The cumulative effect of brushes with man will educate elk, especially the old cows and big bulls who have the advantage of a number of years behind them to contribute to their learning. Figure it out for yourself. If a lead cow is twelve years old—which really isn't all that old for a lead cow—and that cow has bumped into just five hunters a season, she has the benefit of sixty learning situations behind her. If a prime herd bull survives to be six years old, he has thirty experiences under his belt, and no doubt a shot or two sent in his direction to punctuate the experiences. Many elk bump into many more hunters than that in the course of a year, even in places where hunting pressure is deemed moderate. In places with heavy hunting pressure, elk can run into dozens of hunters in the course of a season.

Even for the hunter who heads to distant mountains, all it takes is one or two other hunters walking down a trail tooting their calls all along the way—and the local elk will begin to associate the sounds of a call with a man. All it takes is a hunter skylined on a ridge as he does his calling for an elk to think twice about responding to a call—for fear it's being made by a hunter.

In this day and age, there aren't so many places that a hunter can go to truly get away from all other hunters. It isn't so easy to go beyond the reach of those other hunters to find elk that haven't been educated.

Not too many years ago, before the advent of cow calls and the proliferation of easy-to-blow bugles, elk were easier to fool. Those first cow calls were dynamite, even if you blew a sour note or two. And if you were a good bugler, you could fool just about every bull in the country during the peak of the rut.

Elk are different now. It takes better and wiser calling. It takes more refined tactics. If the elk are smarter, the hunters have to be smarter, too. If the hunters are smarter, even elk that are different can still be fooled.

Elk are creatures of wild, beautiful places, and it's the wise hunter who moves through these places quietly and carefully.

Chapter One

■ ELK TACTICS

What Are the Elk Saying?

Damned if I know what the elk are saying when they talk. And unless you can find some brilliant elk to talk to you in fluent English, French, Chinese, Swahili, or Polish, no other human being can tell you exactly what the elk are saying, either.

Elk talk in elk language, and that's something no person fully understands. They may be able to imitate the sounds. They may be able to guess what the sounds mean. But as to telling you exactly what the elk are saying? Give me a break.

Maybe that's why it always tickles my funny bone when I hear about one call that makes a lonesome mew, another a calf chirp, another a bull chuckle, another an old-bull rasp, another a young-bull squeal, and who knows what all else. That would give you the impression that you really knew what you were imitating and what you were saying. Instead, what all these calls boil down to are common elk sounds—usually called cow sounds—that all elk make and bugles that the bulls make in the rut. But what are we really saying to the elk with each of these things? Who knows? And can we really identify the type of elk we hear by their calls alone? Based on my experiences over the years, you never really know.

This language barrier between man and elk is a fact that really can't be overstated. And despite many lifetimes of experience, and even some clues from the elk, we're still not sure what the elk are telling each other with their calls, or what we're saying to them when we imitate them.

Sometimes I can't help but think humans talking elk language must be something like one of those TV commercials where a person (usually, for some odd reason, an American) tries to ask someone from a foreign country a simple question in their own language. But instead of saying "Where's the nearest bathroom?" the person says something like "How suitcase your mother fits underwear?" And then the person wonders why the foreigner is so confused.

It must be something like that with humans calling elk. What are the elk saying? What are we saying to them?

No human really knows for sure what an elk is saying when he's talking to another elk.

Sometimes, based on the reactions of elk to some of my calling over the years, I must have blown it badly. In my worst nightmare, in fact, I see myself as a hunter just out of range of this magnificent trophy bull elk. And I blow into my call ever so perfectly, trying to say in elk language, "Come on over here and try me, you big old boy!" But instead, I call out, "Run, run for your life! The forest is on fire!"

Of course, that is a worst-case scenario. Suffice it to say that if your current elk calling doesn't send elk scurrying for the local volunteer fire department, you're on the right track, no matter what you're saying in elk language. But if the elk run for an ax, shovel, and bucket every time you make elk sounds, get rid of the call you're using or try to make some different sounds with it.

To fully appreciate the wide range of sounds that elk make, you really ought to spend some time in all seasons in elk country.

Cows and calves talk a lot, for example, when elk are bunched on the winter range. In the crisp, still cold of a January morning, you can hear all kinds of common elk sounds coming from a herd. You'll hear the higher-pitched

Chapter One

ELK TACTICS

calls of the calves, the deeper voices of the cows and bulls, and everything in between. For whatever the reason—and the reason may be nothing more than making small talk—elk talk a lot when they're in groups on the winter range.

If your ears remember the sounds well, you'll be able to pick them out again when you encounter a group of elk getting up on their feet in a bedding area at the end of the day. When an elk herd gets ready to leave the bedding area, they're often very vocal again. Calves talk to their mothers and other calves. Scattered cows talk to each other. The whole herd seems to have something to say. What are they saying? Who knows. Maybe it's nothing more than "It's about time we got up and got some grub."

The onset of the rut, and the bugling of the bulls that goes along with it, opens up another whole repertoire of elk sounds. One of the best learning experiences I've ever had in the wide range of bull sounds out there came on a day when I wasn't hunting at all. Call it one of the perks of living in the heart of elk country. Here, you don't have to hunt everyday. Some days, you can go out and just enjoy the elk and save your hunting for another day.

This day, I wanted to go up in the mountains and simply film some bulls bugling. I got into an area that had scattered timber in a few spots. It had a few little rolling breaks of hills. One little hill was open on one end and had a few trees on the other. I could hear the sounds of elk bugling coming from that area.

It took me quite a while to get close enough to be within filming range. In fact, I didn't get to that spot until about noon. That's after the time most hunters quit for the day because they think all the elk are in their beds and the bugling is over.

What I've found over the years, however, is that elk still bugle in the middle of the day. For some reason, the sound of their bugles doesn't carry so far at that time. Maybe that's because of midday winds, rising hot air carrying the sound off, or whatever. But elk do bugle then, and there were bulls bugling here.

The sound of each bugling bull can be extremely distinctive, and after listening to them for a while, you can pick out each individual.

I got as close to the elk as I dared and made a setup like I was going to do some calling, but instead, I was just going to record elk sounds and watch a couple of open parks. It was about noon, and the first elk I heard was a bull not far off to my right, maybe just 50 to 100 yards away. That bull was

Chapter One

really bugling strong, but was almost bugled out. The stress of so much bugling in the weeks of the rut had caught up to him. All he could make were some hollow-sounding bugles, followed by a couple of grunts.

That bull was answered by a second bull. Then a third chimed in. Then a fourth, fifth, sixth, and maybe more. Over the next two hours, that little piece of real estate back in the Montana mountains came alive with bulls. Based on where the calls were coming from and the various sounds they made, there were anywhere from six to ten bulls out there. Each one was making a different sound. Each bull was calling with a different frequency as well.

One bull had no high pitch in the beginning of his bugle. It was just a series of hollow sounds like you normally hear in the middle of a bugling sequence. That bull, the farthest one out, made his distinctive bugle just seven times over the course of the two hours. The bull to my right was bugling on an average of once every five minutes. He was really working himself up. The frequency of the rest of the bulls' bugling was at all rates in between.

After about a half-hour, three cows walked out from where the nearby bull was bugling. They walked out onto an open hillside, through some trees and up the hill. Another bull came out of the timber walking toward them. He had bugled a couple of times in the timber, but he wasn't excited about what was going on. Eventually, he followed the cows.

Another bull showed up down below me and was coming up through the timber. When I looked closer, I saw another bull was traveling with him, but not close to him. Those two bulls never got any closer to each other than 100 yards, but there was nonstop bugling between them.

I'm sure that, based on the sounds I heard myself that day and in listening to the taped sounds later, there were other bulls in the area, too, that I never saw. How many bulls were out there in total, I don't really know. I don't know how many cows were scattered through the area either.

But I came to realize that, while every elk bugle had the

same overall make-up to it, in a sense, each voice sounded different. The tones were different. The pitches were different. The sequences were different. Even the length of time the elk bugled was different. It was interesting to me, for example, that these bugles very seldom lasted over three seconds in length. Just a few ran as long as five seconds.

Yet in all the elk-calling competitions I've ever watched—and those that I've judged as well—the humans imitating bull elk bugled much, much longer than that. Perhaps when the callers get going, it looks good for the humans doing the listening and puts on a good show, but it doesn't really reflect what I heard that afternoon. If I were to sum up what most of the elk were doing—when you get to the nitty-gritty of elk calling to other elk—the sounds are all very short. They start out high, and they end up low, and they're very basic sounds. Some of the elk may never even break down to the low note. They stay high.

Why do humans trying to imitate elk wind up doing it differently than the elk do themselves? On the one hand, it's man speaking a language he doesn't understand. On the other, it's modern technology. The bugles we have these days allow us to use our air a lot better because of their design. They don't require as much air pressure as it takes for an elk to bugle. The elk run out of air long before we do. As long as you, the human, realize this, it's fine. Unfortunately, some people have tried taking the sounds they hear in these bugling contests out into the field—and they find out they don't have much luck with them. They're speaking a language that the real elk don't understand.

The elk show ended at about 2 P.M. And it ended very abruptly.

Another hunter heard all this bugling in the distance, and he started coming toward it, bugling his way to the top of the ridge behind me. When he spotted me, he walked up and asked, "How's it going." I told him I'd been recording elk sounds, even though we couldn't hear any elk bugling now.

The elk, in fact, had stopped bugling as soon as the hunter reached the ridgetop. When he became visible on the skyline, the elk must have spotted him. From that point on, I

Chapter One

ELK TACTICS

never heard another elk. I never saw another elk, either. From the time the elk saw the hunter, they went silent and went into their hiding mode.

The hunter ended up heading off in another direction. I hiked in the direction I'd seen some of the elk going. I got on a trail where I could see some of their tracks. I followed that trail for an hour and a half, and it led me to another patch of timber farther up the drainage. There, some of the bulls started bugling again. I couldn't see them with my naked eye, and I couldn't pick them up in the distance with my binoculars either.

As I moved closer, they must have spotted me, too. They went silent again. I followed the elk tracks until it was about 5 P.M., far up the drainage from where I'd taped them earlier that afternoon. By then, with evening getting near, the bulls had started bugling again, far ahead of me. I must have been a mile away from them, at least. I'd have had to go across an open area to get to them. If I'd have crossed it, I'm sure they would have spotted me. So I opted for the long walk back home.

One of the lessons that stuck with me from the experience that afternoon was the wide variety of sounds that bulls alone can make. Though they all have the same basic sounds, the variables within those basic sounds are just about endless. Another lesson was how quickly even active bugling can come to an end. Just the physical presence of one hunter on the skyline had stopped the bugling instantly and moved those elk far up the drainage. When elk see somebody, they don't bugle. When they see somebody, they can move long distances.

When we talk about the new elk of today, we're talking about elk that have learned that the presence of man calls for a drastic change in what they're doing. Some people have mistakenly passed all of this off as elk getting call-shy. In truth, it's an expression of elk becoming more people-shy and people-wary, whether that shyness and wariness is due to people making sounds they don't understand or simply showing themselves to elk.

From calf sounds to bull sounds, most elk calls are relatively short in duration, start high, and end low.

In the old days, when elk were less accustomed to human activity and fewer hunters were seeking them, they might have excused some of man's mistakes. Just as the foreigner might have excused the mangling of his native tongue and tolerated the misspoken phrase, the elk might have held in an area and the bulls might have continued their bugling. But now, the new elk, the pressured elk, the man-wary elk, aren't that tolerant.

Elk hunters simply have to be wiser about elk than they used to be. Hunters have to be more precise in their presentation of themselves and their calls. Hunters have to be better elk hunters if they hope to consistently find success with the new elk.

Chapter One

CHAPTER TWO

Where To Hunt

The decision on where to hunt elk is one that shouldn't be taken lightly. If you're hunting within your own state, the closest area isn't necessarily the best choice. The best choice may be half-a-state away. If you're hunting out of state, the state with the cheapest and most available licenses isn't necessarily the best choice either. If you pay a little more, you may get a lot more back out of your hunt.

Much of the decision about where to hunt is a matter of deciding what it is you want out of your elk hunt, of goal setting. If you're interested in nothing short of a record-book bull, you've got to be sure that the area you're hunting is capable of holding such an elk. An area may not produce a lot of elk, but it may provide you with a huge one. If all you want is an elk—any elk—then the number of elk available matters more than the size of the bull. The area may not have ever produced a record-book bull, but it has produced a lot of elk for a lot of hunters. To you, that may be the most important factor.

Hunters also have to decide whether their elk hunting is a one-year, single-season affair or will be an annual event. Hunters are most likely to find consistent success over a number of years if they return to the same area and learn it well. For those hunters, the decision on where to hunt could sometimes be a lifetime commitment. Resident hunters, especially, often return to the same places year after year. They went there with their fathers. They go there with their sons. Uncles, nephews, nieces all make up a part of the hunting party. Their elk area is as near and dear to them as the company of the hunters who join them there.

The best way to find the best area to hunt is to do a lot of talking. If you live far away, that means spending some time on the telephone with fish and game departments, biologists, game wardens, rangers, sporting goods dealers, outfitters, guides, just about anyone who can provide you with firsthand information. Then apply that information to as detailed a set of maps as you can find. If you live nearby, you should visit all those sources, too, plus log some hours on the ground in the off-season. The best information is going to be that which you provide yourself. There's nothing like being there to see an elk area for yourself to really learn about it.

Once you arrive at your hunting area, where do you start? What do you look for? What are you hoping to find? What are the clues that elk leave behind, both when they're in the area and when they're not?

It doesn't take long to realize that elk country is big country—really, really big country. It's country so big that you simply can't cover it all, certainly not in a single season. Sometimes, you can't even cover it all in a lifetime. As a result, just as you have to make careful plans in choosing what state and what general area you plan to hunt in, you've got to have some clues about where to look for elk once you get there.

It's time to pinpoint a little closer where to hunt for elk.

Dissecting a Mountain

Not all mountain ranges are great for elk. Not even all parts of a mountain will hold elk. In fact, perhaps the most daunting task facing any elk hunter is trying to figure out exactly where to hunt.

Think of it this way: Let's say a particular mountain range is forty miles long and twenty miles wide. Let's say the range has a healthy elk herd of four hundred animals. Of those four hundred animals, let's say there's a healthy population of one hundred bulls of all ages. Let's say that ten of those bulls are of trophy stature with huge racks.

If you put your mathematical mind to the equation, you come up with eight hundred square miles in the mountain range. With four hundred elk, if you spread them out equally across the whole mountain range, that means there's one elk for every two square miles. With one hundred bulls, there's one bull for every eight square miles. With ten trophy bulls, there's one trophy bull for every eighty square miles.

With those kinds of numbers, even a hunter in great shape would be hard-pressed to cover enough ground to see more than a few elk in a day. A hunter might cover enough square miles in a week of hard hunting to see a couple of bulls. And, in the course of a season, he might never cover enough ground to spot one of the trophies.

All this takes for granted that elk are evenly spread out across the mountain range. It takes for granted that they're all moving as singles. It doesn't take into account that you might not spot an elk, even though you passed very near to it. And it doesn't really take into account the fact that most elk are traveling in groups, and some of the groups can be quite large.

So let's look at the equation again. Let's say that the four hundred elk are traveling in forty groups of ten elk apiece, though no doubt some elk groups would be much larger in real life. Then each one of those groups would have twenty square miles to call its own. And you'd conceivably have to cover twenty square miles before you bumped into a bunch of elk.

Chapter Two

■ ELK TACTICS

Ridgetops are the highways of the mountains, usually offering the easiest passage over long distances.

All this sounds horribly depressing to a hunter getting his first look at a new mountain range. With vast mountain acreages of very steep up, and very steep down, to traverse, this scenario doesn't offer much hope for a hunter to ever find an elk, or a bull, much less a trophy bull.

But as I said, not all parts of a mountain range or a mountain are created equal. There are some places to look that are far more likely to hold elk than other places. There are some places that are easier to hunt, too. What you've got to do is maximize your efforts by looking in the best places, instead of wasting your time in places that probably aren't holding elk.

Some eliminating of the less likely areas can be done by simple map work. With good topographic maps of a mountain range, and an understanding about how all those squiggly little lines work, you can get a feel for parts of a mountain, or a mountain range. You must make your final decisions, of course, on the ground. And any and all decisions are aided greatly by any firsthand information you can get from others who know the area.

One of the first things I look for when dissecting a mountain is a common, distinct ridge. This main ridge may have several finger ridges coming off of it. In between will be streams or valleys of some sort.

For me, a long, sloping main ridge has always been the best place to start. A ridge like this provides several things for the elk, and for the hunter seeking an elk. It may have a steep drop into a valley at the start, but once you make that short climb, you're on a long ridge that you can hunt and traverse quite easily. These sorts of ridges are often good for taking a hunter a long way without too much of a gain in elevation. For that reason, elk tend to like them, too.

Once you find that ridge, look at it a little closer with a good pair of binoculars or spotting scope. Perhaps the best time to do this is in the early morning or in late evening, when you have low light conditions. At those times of day, the reds and browns show up better and it's easier to spot elk that might be on the ridge. But even if you don't see animals right away, there are other things you should look for. Does the ridge have areas of timber and areas of open meadows? Might there be smaller clearings, scattered among the timber, that you can't see—that your scoping from a distance can't penetrate—but that might offer secluded feeding spots for elk?

It's the ridges that have these things that have consistently been the best elk places for me. They have offered the best starting points for an elk hunter to look for other key pieces of real estate that elk prefer, too. Do some of the small clearings have springs nearby? If there aren't springs, are there seeps that will still offer lush green grass when the other grasses go dry?

It's areas like these that will hold elk. Although elk may not be out feeding in those little clearings throughout the day, they'll be there for the morning and evening feeding times. Elk will move along the ridge. They'll feed out in the small clearings. During the rut, the springs and seep areas will often provide a wallow that bulls will visit as they work off steam.

Now look at the ridge again. Are there areas on the ridgetop, or just off the ridgetop, that hold patches of dense timber? Most often, these patches of dense, dark timber will be on the north side of the ridge, while the south side is

Chapter Two

more open and grassy. It's in that dark timber that the elk will bed during the day. And when all else fails in an elk hunt, you dive into the dark timber and hunt the bedding areas. There are perils to hunting the bedding areas, including blowing the elk clear out of the country if you spook them too badly. But bedding areas are another of the key factors you have to have to make up a good elk ridge. And, sometimes, you hunt them.

Why don't I generally hunt them in the bedding areas? Perhaps the simplest explanation is that elk can move up, over, around, and through the mountains a lot easier than a hunter can. If you leave elk alone in their bedding area, and work them when they're up and feeding, you can get away with a little disturbance. As long as the bedding area is secure, the elk will often stay in the area. But bump them out of their security cover—their bedding areas—and you can move them to places where you just can't follow them, at least not very easily. Elk can move from ridge to ridge and drainage to drainage with ease. It often takes only minutes. Give an elk a few hours to move, and you may find it takes you a day or two to arrive at the same destination.

When dissecting a mountain, you'll quickly notice that the thick patches of dark timber generally grow on the north-facing slopes. The south-facing slopes are generally more open, perhaps with just scattered timber. The north-facing slopes will also generally be more lush in the fall, helped in their water retention by the forest covering and the fact that the sun's rays don't beat directly on them as much. With that lush covering, they tend to play a bigger role for elk in the fall. Besides providing better bedding areas, they also offer elk more security , especially elk that are trying to stay out of the sights of hunters. The south-facing slopes will tend to be more dry in fall. While elk will feed on these open slopes at times, they tend to play a bigger role for elk in spring because the sun will burn the snow off them more quickly and they will be quicker to provide a meal of the first green grasses of the year.

In dissecting a mountain, the next ingredient to look for is

Elk will often move out of the dark timber and into the small open clearings on ridges to feed.

finger ridges off the main ridge. If it's a long main ridge, there may be many finger ridges coming off. Sometimes, finger ridges, especially if they're long ones, will provide good hunting. Other times, elk may bed on the tops of these finger ridges. How do you decide which are good and which aren't worth your time? There's no pat formula, but if you have to go with tendencies, look to the length of the ridge. The longer they are, the better they're likely to be. If they've got good coverage of timber, their chances of being a bedding area are enhanced. If they're relatively open and relatively short, you might catch elk feeding on them from time to time, but usually, for whatever the reason, that type of finger ridge is not worth your effort.

And, just as north-facing slopes tend to have more timber on them, so do the finger ridges that point north and east. Finger ridges that point west or south tend to be more grassy.

Some of my favorite main ridges are ones that aren't straight. If they have a lot of curves, the elk's interest in them seems to increase. And if the elk are more interested in them, it's only logical that elk hunters like me are more

Chapter Two

ELK TACTICS

interested in them as well.

As a prime example, my favorite area is a main ridge that twists and turns for about five miles on its way to the top of the mountain. When it finally reaches the summit, it's the highest point in the area. I've hunted that ridge often and have seen countless elk on it over the years. Certainly, one of the reasons is that it has all the other ingredients that make it a prime area for elk. It has level grassy spots, then patches of timber, then more grass, then more timber. I've bumped into elk on that ridge often in the early morning and late evening as they emerged from bedding areas to feed in those grassy openings.

Another factor to consider in picking a ridge is its width. Ridges narrow, then widen out. Those wide spots may be a half-mile across once you explore them. But it often takes exploring to find these places. Sometimes you can't see them when glassing from the valleys below. It takes a hike to discover them.

One such ridge in my area sits back up at the head of a creek, and it's called Hunter's Home. It's a beautiful ridge that has all the ingredients for a great elk area. There is timber. There are grassy openings. It's just a super setup for elk, with all the things an elk needs. With that in mind, it's no surprise that the ridge has often produced game over the years. If there's a downside to it, it's that Hunter's Home became well-known as an elk area, and, as it became well-known, it has attracted some hunters over the years who didn't know how to hunt it. They moved right in and camped in the open spots on the ridge. They grazed their horses in the grassy openings. They enjoyed the great view. It was, and is, a beautiful place to camp. The activity of the camps, however, alerted all the elk in a fairly wide area. As a result, the elk moved out, and moved out quite a distance. As an elk area, it was ruined by the hunters themselves. Had the hunters camped down low and then worked their way up the ridge in the morning, they would have had excellent hunting. Instead, they tried to camp right in the hunting spot and ruined it for themselves.

In looking at ridges to hunt, in addition to looking for things that will make them attractive to elk, try to eliminate areas that elk aren't going to like. It's a bit like applying pluses and minuses to ridges. Pluses are good. Minuses are strikes against them. If a ridge area is devoid of water, that's certainly one strike against it. If it's extremely steep, that's another strike because really steep areas may hold some game, but not a lot of game. And if there isn't enough cover associated with a ridge to provide security cover for the animals, that could very well be strike three. A ridge with all these problems is definitely out. Odds are it doesn't hold much game.

On the other hand, if—on a long, sloping ridge—you see what appear to be indentations from a distance, that could signify level spots, plateau-type areas that often hold grassy openings or mixed grass and timber. That's a definite plus. If the plateaus look to be large, that's another plus because there is plenty of space for game. Water nearby is a plus, too. If you can see patches of timber at the heads of these plateaus, it's an almost sure bet that these will be bedding areas for elk feeding out on the plateaus. That's a plus, too. There are plenty of good things to say about ridges with plateaus like these. They're definitely worth a hunt.

This system of pluses and minuses is a good way to assess the possibilities of hunting areas. It's also a way to get a handle on things from map work and from long-distance glassing. That saves time when compared to actually hiking every ridge you see in the mountains.

One thing to remember, however, is that it's possible for one missing ingredient to overpower all the rest. So don't get too carried away or be too surprised if a ridge has so many good things going for it, but just doesn't hold elk. Water is a prime example. I know of a number of ridges that have the grassy openings for feeding, they have good timber for bedding areas, and they even have great, broad plateaus. But they don't have water, and there isn't even any water within a reasonable distance. As a result, these ridges are missing a key ingredient and are more likely to be areas that elk will pass through, but won't hold in.

Chapter Two

ELK TACTICS

In formulating your hunting plans, another tendency you should know has to do with creeks that often separate ridges. Sometimes a mountain stream can parallel ridges for miles. But just as the cover on each side of a ridge tends to be different, so does the cover on each side of a creek. The north or east side will most likely have the timber. The south or west side will most likely be more open. For security reasons, the elk will most likely be found on the timbered side during the day. And in early morning or late evening, you might find the elk feeding out into the openings on the other side of the creek.

It should also be pointed out that these tendencies we're talking about deal, for the most part, with lightly hunted to moderately hunted elk. These are the places where elk really want to be. These are the places where elk habitat is best.

Just as lack of water can overpower all other factors in making a place desirable for elk, the security needs of heavily hunted elk can make less-than-perfect habitat seem suddenly the perfect spot to go. For elk, high-security translates into any place that's so nasty that no one goes there, not even when there are many hunters saturating the area. Hard-pushed elk, for example, will move to ridges that are very steep and loaded with timber. In a normal situation, elk wouldn't stay there. Such ridges are just too densely forested, too steep, and too hard for the elk to get around in. But because of the pressure, elk will pull into these high-security spots.

As hunting seasons progress, and more and more elk get pushed, you might look at your mountain a little closer for these places that hunters generally don't go. As more and more elk seek security, these areas sometimes hold good numbers of elk. And wise old bulls will undoubtedly remember the places where they weren't bothered the year before. But for your own sake, remember, too, that these are often also the toughest places to get an elk out of when you get them on the ground. The old saying, "If you hunt them there, you'd better pack a Zippo and a fork, because you'll have to cook them and eat them there," is appreciated best by any hunter who has faced one of those incredibly steep slopes or impenetrable jungles and had to try to get an elk out of them.

For my part, give me the ridges. And if the hunting pressure gets intense, let's move a little farther from the end of the road on those ridges. If you go far enough, most of the time you'll find somewhere where the pressure peters out.

One of my favorite spots for those situations is a long, long, long ridge in the south-central Montana mountains. I'd tell you exactly where it is, but then you'd just add to the pressure, because it is a very, very good ridge. But let me tell you about it anyway, just so you can see what it takes to make a good elk area.

To start with, the main ridge is twenty-five miles long—that's long. There's a good-sized creek that runs along it that eventually winds out of the mountains to the valley below. As you get to the head of the ridge, you find smaller finger ridges, each with its own little creek that feeds the bigger one. Up near its head, the main ridge makes a big S curve as it meanders for its last six or seven miles. Hunting on the top of that ridge is excellent, with all the ingredients that an elk could dream of. But equally good are the finger ridges that come off. These finger ridges are long ones, long enough to hold game of their own.

If I don't find elk on the open top of the main ridge, I can hunt the finger ridges, which are timbered, except for a few, small, grassy openings. One of those finger ridges is three miles long, with good grass on its south side and solid timber on the north. Elk will bed down in the timber during the day and feed out onto the other side in the morning and evening. If there isn't too much hunting traffic up there, the elk will stay out feeding well after daylight in the morning and come out early in the evening for the last meal of the day.

If I don't want to hunt the finger ridges, I can go to the huge bowl at the head of the main ridge. That bowl is about three miles across, with grass and scattered timber on its south face and solid timber on the north. There are several little benches out there, and plateaus, and plenty of water. From the ridge, you can put a pair of binoculars and a spot-

Chapter Two

ting scope to good use and are often able to spot an animal first, before moving in on him. In September, the area has a lot of rubs and a number of wallows. It's a major breeding area and a great spot to hear bugling bulls.

There are number of other good things you can say about this area. It's far enough back in that there isn't much hunter traffic. There are a wide variety of opportunities there, from hunting the bowl, to working the main ridge, to hunting the various finger ridges. It's also at high elevation, which means that it's generally cooler up there in September and early October, which makes it more comfortable for the elk to be up and moving around. At lower elevations, where late summer is sometimes still in full swing, the heat will often put elk to bed much earlier in the morning and delay their emergence from the bedding area later into the evening.

If a hunter is willing to hike back in that far, or is lucky enough to have a horse to carry him that far from the harder-beaten path, the hunting can be excellent. Frankly, most guys don't go that far back in and don't climb that high. But the guys who do are very successful.

But before you lace up your boots, grab a sturdy backpack, and join me, I should tell you about the downside of these way-back-in, high-country, September-October hunts. At that time of year, at those elevations, more than a few hunters have been caught by equinox storms. These early blasts of winter, which inevitably hit the high country in the weeks that surround the official changing of the seasons from summer to fall, can be fierce, and even deadly. The bottom will drop out of the thermometer to far below freezing. Snows can pile up several feet deep. These storms can blow in and keep you pinned down in a tent for several days, easily.

The bad thing about these storms, aside from the fact that you're usually jammed in a too-small tent for a too-long period of time with another guy or guys who haven't showered in a long time, is that you've got to get yourself out of the mountains through all that snow when you're done. Those hikes can be brutal, on man or beast. And if you de-

South-facing slopes will often be more open than north-facing slopes and provide grassy areas for elk to feed.

cide to wait it out for better weather—and often warm, sunny weather will return and may stay nice for weeks—and continue to hunt there, you'll find the elk have left you. Almost invariably with these storms, the elk pull out and move down the mountain. So you might as well pack your packs and slog back down to lower elevations with them.

But rest assured, once you get to the bottom, the same ingredients will be in place for dissecting the mountain to

Chapter Two

pick out the best spots to hunt elk. Elk will still like the ridges, they'll just be a bit lower. They'll still look for heavy timber for bedding areas. They'll still look for open slopes or small grassy openings for feeding. And, if pushed, they'll look for the more impenetrable parts of the country for a good place to hide.

As you get more experience in your chosen piece of elk country—and even if you move to a new hunting area—being able to spot places with just the right ingredients will become easier for you. It will become second nature. In fact, some of the better, old-time, veteran elk hunters I've ever hunted with couldn't really tell me what made a particular place better than others for elk. It just looked good to them. They could spot things that jogged their memory and made them recall other good elk places that looked similar.

For those guys, it was a matter of keeping a notebook of pluses and minuses in their minds. For the rest of us, it may be a bit more formal, at least at the start. So take a pencil and notebook and do some map work before you go, keeping track of the pluses in particular areas. You might even consider taking the notebook along with you when you go, writing things down as you discover them, especially about those places with all the pluses that you want to remember. Then, when you figure you're one of the better, old-time, veteran elk hunters, too, you can throw the notebook away and dissect a mountain for someone else, just by looking at it.

Elk Travel Plans

There's no substitute for an intimate knowledge of your elk hunting area. To carry that one step further, there's no substitute for an intimate knowledge of your hunting area during the hunting season.

As I've said before, elk are creatures of tradition. They seem to remember where prime food sources are located. They know all the water holes. They know what places will be best for them in particular seasons. Elk herds summer in the same places year after year. They winter in the same places. With just a smidgen of variability due to the annual weather pattern, you can pretty much predict where they're going to be.

All of these places are linked together by a network of trails that are traditional as well. Unraveling that trail system and knowing where trails lead is part of the intimate knowledge that a hunter gains only by hiking the trails. If you hike enough trails, you'll paint yourself a better picture of where you're most likely to find elk.

A number of years ago, I hunted with a friend who had that kind of intimate knowledge of an elk herd that fed on the lush green grass on the banks of a big reservoir. It was a fall feeding pattern that repeated itself every year as the higher slopes dried out in the late summer heat while the grass along the reservoir stayed green. The feeding pattern continued into the fall until the snow started falling.

The friend had told me about this elk herd before, going into detail about how the elk would spend the night in the lowlands. He talked about bugling bulls. He told about how the elk would breed there in the cool autumn nights.

But when it came time for an early-morning hunt on these elk, he drove his pickup truck in the opposite direction from the reservoir. Instead of going down, he opened a ranch gate and started driving up and away from the lush green fields. He drove up. And up. And up. And up.

Finally, he stopped the pickup at the base of the highest ridge in the area, perhaps two to three miles away from the reservoir. By then, it was full light. By then, I was sure, our early-morning chances at these reservoir elk were over. But the friend pulled out his binoculars, aimed them down the slope toward the reservoir, and said simply, "Here they come."

Far below, visible only with binoculars, was a string of elk starting to climb a hard-beaten path up from the lush fields below. Even at a great distance, you could tell that the path the elk were following was well worn. It had been used a lot, by countless elk, for decades—probably since the reservoir was formed.

The path that these elk would follow was easily two-plus

■ *ELK TACTICS*

Elk herds may follow the same paths, year after year, as they migrate from summer range to winter range.

miles long. It made an incredible vertical climb toward the ridge where we were standing. It would take those elk perhaps an hour to make the climb to the ridge, which held their daytime bedding areas. And along the way, when you looked close at the elk, you could sometimes see their mouths open and their tongues protruding as they carried a night's feeding worth of grass in their bellies up the long slope.

We bumped elk throughout that day as we hunted the high heavy forest on that ridge, but we didn't get one. The lessons the hunt taught me far exceeded the value of any elk I might have taken. I learned elk will sometimes go a long, long, long way between their feeding and bedding areas. They'll do a lot of climbing, too. The paths that they follow from one place to another are predictable. And if you unravel the travel plan, you can sometimes turn a brief morning encounter down low into a day full of chances at those elk further along the way.

Unraveling elk travel plans generally involves two different types of trails. And each of those trail types is important, depending on the season. The story about those reservoir elk is a classic example of a feeding trail. Tracks and trails that go up and down a mountain are generally made by elk going from bedding areas to feeding areas, and back again. Trails that go around mountains are usually migration trails, taking elk seasonally from one type of habitat to another.

Feeding trails are generally not long-distance routes. They may stretch for a mile or maybe two or three, but their main feature is elevation change. Elk like to bed high, if they can. The good feeding areas are often low, whether those feeding areas happen to be lush green grass (like it was for the reservoir elk) or perhaps grain fields.

One of the tastiest elk—and certainly one of the fattest—that I ever shot was a six-by-five bull I called in once out of his bedding area. That bedding area was on a high slope just above a hailed-out barley field. The hail damage was so bad that the farmer couldn't harvest the crop. But the elk fed down into that field every evening and fattened themselves on that barley all night long. After a month of feeding on grain, that elk was fat. And when his steaks hit the table, I found out that grain-fed elk is pretty hard to beat.

Migration trails are longer than feeding trails. Year after year, elk travel these same routes going from winter range to summer range in spring and early summer. Then they hike them back again when the snow and cold forces them to lower south-facing slopes in late fall and early winter.

While late-season rifle hunters are the major beneficiaries of the migration trails as far as taking elk from them, every hunter can make use of them. These migration trails are usually the easiest way to cover ground in the mountains. Not only do they provide clear footing for elk and elk hunter alike, they tend to follow land contours that are the easiest travel routes. And these trails often run for many miles, all of them good miles of trail.

Invariably, it takes a while for young hunters or novice elk hunters to discover this easy-travel aspect of the migration trails. I can remember learning it the hard way myself, time and time again. I'd look across a big valley or a canyon

Chapter Two

ELK TACTICS

and think I could make better time if I just went straight across it. I'd look at a high ridge and think I could get over the top faster if I went straight up the slope. Even in my young and athletic stage of life, doing it this way took a toll on me physically. And it always took a long, long time, even if only because I had to keep stopping to catch my breath. I've learned over the years that it's better to follow the contours of the land and the trails that invariably follow those contours. Over the years, the elk have gotten pretty smart about taking the easiest way to get around in the mountains and wise elk hunters have found it easier to follow the lead of the elk.

If you do have to make an elevation change either up or down, and it doesn't look like there's a trail that follows the contour of the land directly, it's still best to learn from the elk. You can sometimes work your way from trail to trail and gradually zigzag your way up and down the slopes. Even that is better than the direct route—believe me.

Another benefit of this zigzagging between trails is that eventually you may hit a trail with tracks on it—sometimes a lot of tracks, sometimes a few. The tracks will help you determine what's going on at the time with the elk in the area. Long-traveling tracks will sometimes go for miles without a break in stride, telling you that elk are on the move from one area to the next. Sometimes the tracks will lead you toward key clearings where elk will feed. If the tracks peter out toward the clearing, the elk have obviously spread out to feed. If you go across the clearing by the easiest route, you can often pick up a well-defined trail again as the elk moved on. If you get over there and find no tracks on the trail and go a bit higher and find no tracks, it's an indication that those elk went to that open meadow, fed, and are bedded down straight up the hill. Elk will often bed on little benches above an open park. If that's the scenario you suspect, the best approach is to make a big circle to try to get above the bench and hunt down toward where you think the elk will be. It might be a temporary or permanent bedding area. Some bedding areas may be used just one night. Others may be used night after night. Either way, if there's sign there, you've added a key trail to your elk knowledge for hunts in the future.

Of course, snow cover helps on an elk trail. It's so much easier to tell how long ago tracks were made. You also have the benefit of looking up ahead and seeing what trails the elk are using. With a good pair of binoculars, you can read tracks on a trail from a long distance or glass distant open parks to see which trails are being used.

Once upon a time, a friend and I were tracking elk in the snow, following those tracks on a trail that led straight up the mountain. It was a trail that led from a feeding area to a bedding area somewhere up the slope. In the snow, the going was relatively slow and it took us until about noon before we came near to where that bedding area was likely to be. Finally, as the elk entered a patch of timber, the two bulls split up. I told my partner to take the high track, and I took the low.

It looked like that lower track might drop into the bottom, but I knew the trails in that country well enough that I remembered there was a little bench out there ahead of me. As I worked slowly along, walking down a finger ridge toward the bench, I began to realize that there was a pretty good chance of seeing that elk ahead of me, because I was hunting down on him. I was going slow and glassing and not making noise. But I couldn't see the bull. Finally, I reached a point where I could smell the bull. He was nearby someplace. I just couldn't see him.

What I didn't know right then was that the elk had apparently lain down just off to the side of the finger ridge. But despite my slow approach, the bull spotted me before I spotted him. And he took off. I walked over to where the bull had bedded and was standing right in his bed when I heard a sound. The snow had a little crust on it that day, and it was just a little crunchy. I could hear the crunch of footsteps coming toward me through the trees. Those footsteps were made by the other bull, who had lain down perhaps five hundred yards away. My partner had jumped that bull and he was coming over to his partner, knowing the trail he

Chapter Two

ELK TACTICS

would follow and the area where he would bed.

By the time I saw that second bull, I ended up shooting at him at almost point-blank range, right from the first bull's bed. And I missed him, blowing a big chunk of hair out of his hide. Quickly chambering another round as the elk turned and ran, I hit him with the second shot, right in the back of the head, at twenty yards, as he was running away.

Knowing the trails through an area can pay off in other ways, too. Another time, a friend and I were once again out hunting in snow. It was a couple of hours after daylight, and we spotted a bull far away across an open park. It took us almost two-and-a-half hours to reach the spot where the bull had entered the timber. As we followed the bull and began dropping into a canyon, we spotted another bull that came out into an opening and went back into the same patch of timber that the first bull had entered.

We used a tactic that I have used often, with one hunter taking a high trail and the other hunter going low and following the elk. In this case, my friend took the low trail and had the better chance of taking one of the bulls. So we arranged it that he had the best opportunity to sneak up on one. Alone, he followed the trail the elk were following. One hunter always makes less noise than two. And my accompanying him on that trail would have only increased the chances that the elk would detect us before we detected them. I told my friend that I would follow on a parallel trail that I knew of, a distance up the slope. My friend probably wouldn't be able to see me. But I would travel slowly and be somewhere above him, and somewhere behind him. Somewhere up ahead, he should find the bulls bedded down. It was the perfect spot for it.

We were slowly working along, and I was waiting to hear that telltale gunshot from somewhere below, somewhere up ahead, that would signal my friend's success.

Eventually, the shot came. My friend had jumped one of the bulls and shot it. He never saw the second bull, but the shot must have startled it from its bed. As I waited on that upper trail, that second bull came toward me. And I was

There's nothing like snow to help unravel elk travel plans, and perhaps to help find the elk making those tracks.

ready for him. He finally came into view, and I got that bull, too. Both were nice six-points. And both were bagged because we knew the trail system well enough that we could split up. My friend took his bull off the lower trail. I got mine when the second bull tried to pass through on the upper trail.

Before you get the impression that I've got all these elk figured out, or that these Montana elk are easy, or that I know all the trails, or that I can predict exactly where an elk

ELK TACTICS

is going to go at any given time, let me set you straight. Anytime you hunt elk, you're in a bit of a guessing game as to where the elk are going to be and what they're going to do. What you're trying to do is to second-guess the elk, based on what you know about the animals and what you know about the trail network in the places they live.

Rest assured, there have been plenty of failures. In truth, most of the time it's the elk that comes out the winner. Maybe it's because you tend to remember the times you came out on top that the stories sound so great and the hunts all sound so easy. But I fully realize that what we're involved with here is a game of playing the odds against those elk and trying to tip those odds in your favor.

To some extent, you always guess. Sometimes you guess right. Sometimes you don't. In the story of the high bull and the low bull above, I honestly thought in my own mind that those two bulls were going to try to come back out of that timber the same way that they went in. They didn't know that we had entered the timber behind them. They knew the area that they had passed through was a safe area. With that in mind, if we jumped them, they'd likely try to circle back. But, just as easily, those elk could have done the opposite to us. Sometimes, the elk run out of the timber as fast as they can in the other direction. That bull of mine certainly had that option. And he did take the higher trail, which he hadn't traveled before. But knowing the trail system gave me a leg up on him. That knowledge was just enough to improve my odds and wound up bagging me a bull.

Playing the odds with your knowledge of the trail system goes beyond analyzing feeding trails. It also comes into play with migration trails.

In elk country, you often hear about hunters who stay home, or hunt birds, or go after ducks, or chase antelope or deer during the early part of the elk season. They won't go after elk until they get a little weather—some snow, some cold, and hopefully a little melting and freezing to create a crust—that's going to start the elk migrating toward their winter ranges.

These are hunters who know the migration trails and the places along them where elk are likely to be caught on their travels from summer range to winter range. By waiting for the onset of wintry weather, these hunters also know that they're more likely to be hunting for migrating elk, rather than elk that are native to a particular drainage. That can make a big difference in locating elk and in predicting where you can ambush them.

The tracks left by native elk, for example, will stay in that drainage. They might be a little higher or a little lower, depending on weather and snow conditions. But you don't need to think any further about it. Their trails are mostly vertical, up and down the mountain from feeding areas to bedding areas. But migrating elk might be heading toward a winter range twenty or thirty miles away. The horizontal, traveling trails that they leave behind in the snow may literally result in a case of here yesterday, gone today, or here today and gone tomorrow.

For these migrating elk, you need a pretty good knowledge of where the elk trails are coming from and where the trails are leading to. For migratory elk, you might see elk or the tracks they left behind in one drainage today, then if weather conditions are right, they can be gone by shooting time tomorrow morning. You might improve your odds by trying to catch them in the next drainage along the trail tomorrow. Or two drainages down. Or three or more.

If you add hunting pressure into the traveling equation, elk can move a long, long way in a relatively short period of time. Your odds of hitting their trail and being able to follow them and walk them down are slight. Your odds improve if you can leap ahead of the migrating elk and try to outguess them. Given enough knowledge of their trails and enough time to locate where the elk are in their migration, you can head them off. But it takes some knowledge and sometimes, some mobility in tough snow conditions. If possible, it's best to get ahead of the migrating elk and hunt back toward them. That way they can bump into you.

Intimate knowledge of elk travel plans can help you in other ways, too. They can help you especially when you get

Chapter Two

ELK TACTICS

Knowing where elk will go when pushed by hunters can help you set up an ambush somewhere along the way.

into fresh snow conditions, where there aren't fresh tracks to guide you as to where you should go or to show you exactly where the trails might be.

The best example of that happened just this winter during the annual late elk hunt at Gardiner. The hunt is limited to special permit holders only. Those permits are awarded each August in Montana. And a specified number of hunters are given specified time periods in which they're allowed to hunt. This year, my son Ryan was one of those permit holders.

The elk that are being hunted are almost all migratory. They're on their way from summer ranges in the high country, where they spend the summer and fall, to winter ranges located farther down the Yellowstone River valley. It's a relatively long migration of twenty or more miles for many of the elk. And there are hunters all along the way in two two-day time periods each week, trying to trim back the herd's cow numbers, or in four-day time periods in search of a bull.

The paths that the elk follow are the same ones that have been used for centuries, at least. And outfitters who guide clients in search of those elk, and hunters like Ryan and me who live nearby, are well aware of those paths and rely on them when there are tags to be filled.

This year, we used both the outfitters and the paths to our benefit. Knowing that outfitters would push the elk along the migration trails as clients filled their tags at first light, Ryan and I moved farther down the migratory corridor. Even though snow covered the trails, we knew where they were from previous hunts in the area and from watching the elk move through. We positioned ourselves where two prominent trails cut across the face of a mountain, taking a position between them. By being in just the right spot, we could cover both trails and get a shot at an elk no matter which trail the animals took. True to form, the outfitters' clients filled tags at first light on a migrating herd and thinned the number of elk down quite a bit. But as that herd moved on, they eventually came to us on one of the trails. There were still a number of cows left and a number of bulls with them. Ryan got his shot, bagged a big cow, and was able to fill his antlerless elk permit. As I said, it sometimes sounds so easy when you play the odds and know the trails where the elk are likely to go.

In looking back on my elk hunting over the years, it's hard to overemphasize the importance of knowing your hunting area well and the travel plan that the elk have worked out within it. That knowledge makes so much difference in how you move through the area, how easily you move through, and where your odds are best to find an elk.

By sizing up a mountain or mountain range, dissecting its many parts, and knowing the travel plan within it, you've

Chapter Two

already taken huge steps in finding where elk are likely to be. Without finding the elk, you'll never be able to call them in. You won't be able to predict where they'll go when pressured. You won't be able to fine-tune your approach toward resident elk who live in an area or elk that are just passing through.

All that's left is the need to read the signs that the elk leave behind and to assess what the elk are doing in the area. If you know elk habits in a particular season, and read the signs that they leave behind, you'll have cut the odds further of getting an elk within bow range or rifle range. And you'll have set the stage further for becoming both a successful elk caller and a successful elk hunter.

Reading Sign

There's nothing like a steaming pile of elk droppings on a cold day to let you know that an elk has just been standing there. Tracks on the edge of a stream with the water still trickling into them are good, too. And there's a lot to be said for a crisp, snowflake-free track when the snow is coming down hard. It's easy to follow tracks in the snow and know, for sure, which direction an elk has headed. A warm elk bed reeking with scent is easy to identify as a place where an elk has just been napping. And elk hair stuck to the sap of a freshly rubbed tree is a dead giveaway, too.

Some elk sign is just plain easy to read. But if there's no snow on the ground, or no elk hair, or no steaming piles, frankly, it's not so easy to decipher the telltale leavings of bull, cow, and calf elk. Yet being able to read sign is another critical aspect of elk hunting. You've got a huge leg up on the competition if you can assess what's going on around you in elk country—and, better yet, if you can tell when that activity took place.

Elk in the late summer and fall have certain things they do that leave sign behind. Bulls rub their antlers against trees and tear up bushes and saplings. Bulls wallow during the rut. Bulls, cows, and calves may visit mineral licks. Elk have their various types of food that they key in on, all at particular times of the year. And, of course, they go through their daily routines of moving to and from bedding areas and feeding areas.

In the process, elk leave behind the basic ingredient that all sign-readers must be able to assess—tracks. Tracks will take you where elk go. They won't always tell you when they went there, however.

The first thing you have to understand about tracks is that many of the ones you see may have been made at night, or at least not during normal hunting hours. Elk, especially elk who know there's a hunting season going on, tend to be extremely nocturnal. They may wait to get on their feet until the last light of day. They may be well on their way back to their beds as the first light is returning the following morning. Tracks in the snow are perhaps the easiest to age, because new snow covers old tracks and tracks in the snow tend to weather and look old quickly. But even without snow to help you along, tracks in the dirt or mud can also be read for age. If there's a rule of thumb I follow, it's that tracks that look really fresh most usually are fresh, especially in the fall. During those days of autumn in the high country, where you most often have frost every morning, the moisture in the ground comes up as the day warms. That rise in temperature and moisture will push the dirt up and back down again and make an elk track look old quickly. If you have a rain come through—even if it doesn't dump a lot of moisture—this, too, will soften the crisp edges of a fresh track and make it look old. Even the wetting and drying action of a heavy dew will flatten out a new track.

But the truth of the matter is that just as long as you're not looking at ancient tracks, even less-than-brand-new tracks will tell you a lot about the elk that you're chasing. They tell you that elk have been using a particular elevation. They tell you that elk have been in a particular drainage. They can lead you to feeding areas. And with a bit closer look there, you can determine what the elk have been eating.

Droppings that the elk leave along the way can provide you with some keys as well. When elk start eating dry grass or dry forage, their droppings become harder and are very much in pellet form. If they've been eating green grass, their droppings are softer and more flattened—they're almost more of a patty shape than a pellet shape. If the droppings have a glaze on them, even if they're not warm, that usually means they're pretty fresh. After the sun has been on them for a while, the glaze dries and they become more dull in appearance and look older.

Wandering tracks of many elk fanning out usually means that elk are in a feeding mode. Elk traveling single-file means they're in more of a traveling mode. The feeding mode is the thing you're looking for. That feeding mode may take place in the timber. It may take place in clearings. In either case, look around for what the attraction is that has started the elk feeding.

Elk seem to have the ability and desire to key in on a food source and to all but abandon other items that would be good elk food, too. In my part of Montana, the best example is a mountain mushroom that appears in the high country toward the end of August and into early September. When these mushrooms are out, the elk herds will spread out in the timber and hunt them hard. The only sign they leave behind, aside from their spread-out, wandering tracks, are little indentations on the forest floor where they've poked their noses in to nip off the mushrooms just below ground level. Other times, they'll feed heavily on flower tops that have gone to seed. These seedpods must be a high-nutrition item indeed because the elk search them out hungrily, and you'll go to clearings where the tops of all the stalks have been neatly nipped off. Then, they might go back on a diet of mountain grass for a number of days. Then, they might go to eating newly emerged needles off pine trees. They might get into a patch of dwarf huckleberries and crave their red berries. Or rose hips. Or a particular type of weed or shrub. I've seen signs of elk eating all these things as the seasons change from summer to fall to winter.

The importance of being able to read sign about what the elk are eating is that it provides another piece of the puzzle

Big wallows may be used by more than one bull and may be used for many years, while small wallows may be used by one bull for one year.

Chapter Two

in trying to figure out where you'll find them. The mushrooms, huckleberries, or flower seedpods may all be in season at just one elevation in the mountains at the particular time you happen to be there. The elk might not come back to that particular spot where you found their feeding activity, but you'll be able to identify other areas that have the same type of food. Knowledge of that food source will increase your odds of finding elk there.

Another thing to consider about reading sign on the food the elk are eating is that it often isolates elk to a particular elevation. If all the dwarf huckleberries are at an elevation of six thousand to seven thousand feet and the elk are gorging themselves on them, for example, then you know the part of the mountain where you should concentrate your efforts. You want to look and keep looking for the particular food source, at a particular elevation, that the elk are using the most. Those are the places you're most likely to find elk sneaking out of their bedding areas toward evening or wandering back toward their beds in the early morning.

Once again, experience in your chosen hunting area will become invaluable. Over time, over the years of hunting the same area at about the same time, you'll get to know what the elk are likely to be feeding on. You'll know the areas where that food source is most likely to be found. And, by then, pretty much all you'll have to do is find the fresh tracks, find the fresh scats, and you'll know exactly where the elk will be. Once elk become accustomed to a particular food source, at a particular time, they can be patterned. They are creatures of habit. And they're not just hiking around to see more country and to leave their tracks behind.

So what happens if you hunt the same area, at the same time of the year, and don't see tracks, and don't see the elk eating their favorite food? That's when you've got to look to outside factors—if you hadn't noticed them before that. For some reason, the food source isn't there in that particular year. Perhaps it's a wetter year. Perhaps it's dryer. Perhaps spring frosts killed off the flowers and there weren't seedpods or berries. Or perhaps there was an early cold snap that changed things around. Somehow, the vegetation cycle has been altered from the cycle both you and the elk have grown accustomed to. The food appeared earlier, or later. The elk have moved on to something more in season or more in abundance. So get back to your sign reading and figure it out. The experience will add one more variable to your cache of knowledge that can be applied not just this year, but in some future year when you run into similar conditions.

As you follow elk tracks and wander through feeding areas, I should tell you that I've always had some very little helpers to help me age the things I saw. These little helpers are mountain spiders. Now I can't really tell you how many kinds of spiders there are in the mountains where I hunt. I can tell you that there are a bundle of them. And I can tell you that they spend more than a little of their time spinning webs. These webs seem to appear in short order and in abundance in the mountains.

These webs also invariably stretch across elk trails. In the morning light, especially when there's a little dew on them, these webs glisten in the sun and are easy to spot. If you're hiking an unused game trail, you'll feel the webs hit you across the face and see them pull on your clothing. And, I'm sure, the same thing happens to the deer and elk that use the trails. So it's only logical that trails which are totally web-free or have few webs on them have had deer or elk using them, and probably pretty recently. Trails that still have webs across them in abundance probably haven't been used in quite a while. In fact, if I see a trail with a lot of webs, I'm sure that no elk have passed there for at least three or four hours and perhaps a lot longer.

Those spider webs were the inspiration for a low-tech, low-budget alternative to the commercial trail-checkers that you can purchase or rig for yourself to determine elk trail usage. Instead of packing cameras, rigging triggering devices, or using commercial light-beam sensors to monitor elk trails, I just packed a spool of sewing thread. When I was hunting an area for more than a day or two, I'd put some threads across it, just like one of those spider webs. I

Chapter Two

ELK TACTICS

Elk rubs can be found at any time of year, but their use is generally restricted to the weeks before and during the rut.

didn't tie them off hard to bushes or trees on either side of the trail, just pretty much draped them across the foliage. I'd put the threads about waist high, so that small animals and even coyotes could pass underneath them. But anything big, be it an elk or a deer, would run into them and pull them out. When I saw the thread pulled out the next day, I knew there was game passage on the trail. If I checked out the tracks, I could tell what it was. By putting the threads up in the evening, I could check the next morning and learn if there was night-time use. By putting up threads in the morning and returning later in the day, I could tell if there was day-time use.

For no more than the price of a spool of thread—or, if you are sneaky and know where your wife's stash is located, for no price at all—you can fine-tune your knowledge of the use patterns of animals in your area.

Some trails won't lead to feeding areas. They may lead to other features that attract elk, like mineral licks. Most of them are even natural. One of mine was not.

I was out one time during the summer, just hiking and checking out the elk area I was going to hunt that fall. Living out here, where I can do that type of thing, is a big advantage for learning elk country, and it's even better if you live close to the area like I do. That summer, in an open meadow, I came across what I classified at the time as a natural mineral lick. There was water there. The ground was dug up in an area about twenty yards across. And, like many mineral licks, it was dug down fairly deep into the ground. Close to the lick was some water, a stream that went past. It was a beautiful thing and obviously a real elk magnet.

From all directions, trails led to the lick. Fresh elk tracks were in abundance. I thought to myself that this was going to be a dandy place to find elk once hunting season arrived. I don't think I ever shot an elk right there. But it was always a place I kept in the back of my mind over the next few hunting seasons. About five or six years later, I happened to be talking to an old-timer about elk hunting and mentioned the spot. From what he told me, I could only laugh—at the lick and at myself. It turned out that my mineral lick was actually a spot where an old outfitter had been dropping rock salt over the year. The outfitter was long since out of business. And it had been a long time since any rock salt had been dropped there. But enough salt had leeched into the ground that the elk were still coming back to the spot. They were eating the dirt, trying to get the salt out of it.

That rock salt lick was just one of the things that the old-timers had used to hold elk in an area. They knew that while food and water were the basics of elk needs—and these were there with the open meadow and the creek—an added attraction like a lick made the spot all that much better. Back in the old days, that kind of thinking wasn't

Chapter Two

frowned upon. It was a normal piece of business. And it did attract elk, even long after the old outfitter was gone.

Not all mineral licks are man-made, of course. There was an area I hunted for a couple of years back in the Bob Marshall Wilderness, of northwestern Montana, that was famous for its mineral licks. These licks, too, attracted elk to the area; they chewed up the mud to gain minerals from it. And, once upon a time, I figured they'd provide a pretty sweet ambush for a hunter with a bow and arrow. So I positioned myself within bow-shot range of the better part of a mineral pond that was being frequented by elk.

But I found out two things on that hunting trip that made me less fond than perhaps I should have been about positioning myself near a lick for elk. The first problem was the elk themselves. The lick I was watching was out in a meadow, not too far from some timber. And the elk did come. But they came in ever so slowly. They came in ever so warily. They came in as far away as they could have from the timber where, naturally, I was in hiding, waiting for them. And they came in so high strung and wired that by the time my bowstring twanged and the arrow reached where the elk had been standing, the bull had leaped several feet away and watched the arrow as it whizzed past. But it was the other part of the lick situation, more than anything else, that discouraged me further from setting up an ambush there. That was when I looked a little more closely at the mud at the edge of the lick and then at the trail I was standing next to as I stood at my ambush point. Both in the mud, and in the trail, were some formidable grizzly bear tracks. No wonder the elk were so wired. It seems that grizzlies realize, too, that mineral licks attract elk. As a result, mineral licks in grizzly country tend to attract some attention from grizzlies, too. As a result, they didn't need much close attention from me.

The prospect of a grizzly sneaking in on you unnoticed is a very real possibility in elk country. Or a black bear. Or a mountain lion. For that reason, you should always approach places like mineral licks with care and your eyes wide open.

Confrontations with predators should always be avoided, if at all possible. But you've got to realize, too, that places like mineral licks do act, to a degree, as elk magnets. And if the elk are there, you're probably going to find yourself there as well, at some point in your elk hunting career. Suffice it to say that it has always been my opinion that if a predator bigger than I am wants to stake out a mineral lick, I say let him have it. I'll find another spot without the giant tracks or the bear that made them.

Rubs are another sign that elk are using an area, especially during the weeks leading up to and during the rut of late August, September, and early October. In truth, bull elk rub trees at other times of the year, as well. But the surge of hormones that accompanies the rut just seems to make them rub more.

You can't really assess a rub from a distance. From far away, it's sometimes easy to confuse an elk rub with the work of porcupines, who also do more than their share of defacing our forests. If it's an elk rub, you'll often find hair that was left behind, clinging to the sap. Also, elk make rubs no higher than they can reach with their heads and antlers. It would be wrong to assume that a rub twenty feet up a tree is made by a really, really, really big bull elk. It would be just as wrong to assume that a rub just a foot of the ground was made by his midget cousin.

Elk rubs will also differ with the season. Sometimes, elk will only rub on one side of the tree. Other times, they'll completely annihilate the tree. If the tree is annihilated, broken off, its bark in shreds, and the carnage is all around the tree, that's a sign it was done during the rut. Bull elk rub violently during the breeding season. If the rub is just on one side of a tree and the tree hasn't been worked over a lot, the rub was probably made during another time of the year. Elk are constantly rubbing their antlers and heads on trees. Just finding rubs doesn't mean that the rub was created during the rut. It depends on what type of rub it is.

Once you've got a guess about what time of year the rub was made, look a little closer and try to pinpoint its age more closely. As a rub ages, the bark of the tree tends to curl up. Does the rub have a green tint to it? That would mean it was relatively fresh. If it's a pine tree, what about the sap of the tree, the pitch? Usually on a fresh rub, the pitch has a yellow cast to it. Older rubs will be whiter and more glazed.

If the rubs are fresh, that obviously means that there are elk actively using the area. But even old rubs aren't bad. Bulls will often return to the same areas each year during the rut. So, if you find an area with rubs, plan to return there to hunt yourself.

Bull elk display areas are another thing to look for. They are usually made on dry ground on a gentle, grassy slope in the timber. Bulls will tear up the grass and paw the ground over an area up to about ten feet square, and they'll urinate in it. In some ways, it's just a giant version of a white-tailed deer scrape. The ground will be torn up somewhat, and sometimes their bed, where they'll lie down, stretch out, and display to any passing cows, will still be evident and have the smell of elk in it. The display areas will exist until rain or snow removes them. Basically, what a display area tells you is that cows and bulls have been working the patch of timber you're in and you're in a good spot for hunting. The bulls I have witnessed making these display areas have made them during the day. Moose also make dry ground display areas, but that's another story. Also, your dog will try to roll in a moose display area—they have an odor all their own.

Wallows are another sign that elk are using the area. You can find wallows at any time of the year. But they're only active during the rut, when bulls will use them to work off steam, cool their hormone-charged bodies, and make themselves look mean.

If you find a wallow in the off-season, it may look like nothing more than a big puddle, or even a deep indentation in the earth without water. They're normally found anyplace where you have a moist area. It might be a little spring. It might be a swampy area. Some wallows are located in the timber. Others are found in open parks and

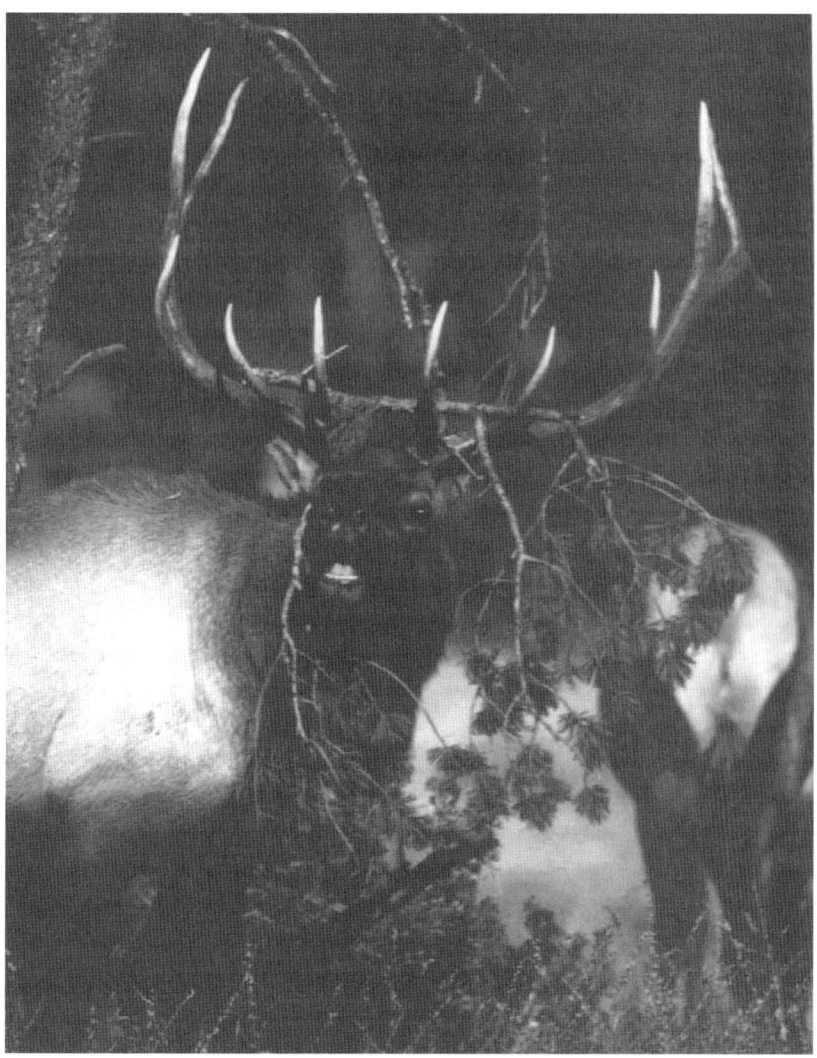

Bull elk will tear off branches and rake tree trunks with their antlers as they work off steam during the rut.

meadows. Sometimes, there might be two wallows in the same park. Some are barely bigger than an elk. Some are so large that you can't even jump across them. Some are relatively shallow, others may look deep.

The size and depth of wallows indicates how much use they've seen. Some shallow wallows may be used by just one elk. A big, deep wallow may be a site that many bulls

Chapter Two

ELK TACTICS

use. Just as wallow use differs in terms of the numbers of elk using it, so does the frequency of that use. Some wallows are used year after year by elk. Others may be a one-year phenomenon. It's those every-year wallows, of course, that can become a key to hunting success year after year. But even then, wallows may not be used every day. Or they may be used more than once a day. There's just no set rule that applies to all.

One thing that does remain fairly constant is when wallow use begins. In my part of elk country, that use begins in the middle of August and may continue into the month of October. And the way wallows are used is pretty much a constant, too. Bulls will roll in them. They'll paw the dirt around them and the mud in them. They'll rake and dig up the grass and reeds and any other vegetation around them. They'll hook and thrash and roll, and by the time they're done, they're dripping with mud and littered with loose vegetation.

As far as the effectiveness of making a stand near a wallow in hopes of ambushing an elk, that, too, has great variability. I made my own little study one time and watched two different wallows—big wallows. Elk used them quite frequently. There's nothing more exciting than looking at a wallow and seeing that the water is muddy and the grass is flattened down and there is mud scattered. That's when the adrenaline starts to flow because you figure the elk might be standing nearby looking at you. But in my case, that has never happened.

I stayed on one wallow that I was sure the elk were using every day. I took a decoy with me and decided to stay on the wallow until dark. That meant I'd have to walk back two hours in the dark to where my truck was parked. But I was ready for that. I had determined earlier that the wallow was being used sometime toward evening. So I got there at 3 P.M. I got into position and set myself up for a shot. I sat there for three hours and never saw an elk, never heard an elk, never, of course, got a shot at an elk. Maybe they were using it at night. I sat there from 3 P.M. until dark and never heard an elk, never saw an elk. I had plenty of opportunity to think to myself that perhaps the wallow was being used at night, and not in the evening.

Anyway, that's the last time I ever tried that myself. To me, that was too inactive. I guess I just don't have the patience to be a stand hunter. After I sit for a length of time, I figure I've sat for long enough—especially when there's no elk to be heard. I'd rather get back on my feet and go see some country, read some sign, and find some elk. Another thing you have to remember is that a wallow isn't used anymore if the elk that happened to use it, or made it, gets taken by a hunter. A lot of times, when that happens, another elk may not come in and use it. In fact, the wallow may go dead.

That doesn't mean other hunters haven't ambushed elk at wallows. In a way, I admire those people. They've got a lot of patience to sit. And some of those sitters take elk. There was one fellow from Florida who gave me a call at my office in Gardiner and wanted to show me an elk he took off a wallow. He had been hunting near Helena, Montana, and went so far as to rent a car, put the antlers in the back, and drive the nearly 200 miles to Gardiner just to show me. It was an exceptionally nice bull, and he had to tell me his story.

The man was hunting a wallow and opted to stick with it. Finally, the bull came in and he shot at it with his bow, missed, and the bull ran off. The man pulled out his cow call, brought the bull back in, and nailed it with the second arrow. The man said he just wanted to shake my hand for making that cow call because, without it, he said, he'd never have gotten his elk.

That kind of thank-you is always appreciated, but the lesson the man left me with is that persistence and patience were what really paid off for him. Patience is a wonderful attribute, if a guy can maintain it. The bulk of us—myself included—can't always maintain it long enough. But we should keep trying. The man's story was a good reminder, too, that a hunter is often pretty jittery on his first shot. By the second shot, he calms down much more. If, of course, the elk presents you with a second shot. That doesn't happen very often.

Chapter Two

ELK TACTICS

In these photos from Billy Hoppe, you can see the bull elk that got stuck in the mud in a wallow and was hopelessly trapped until a horseman put a rope around his antlers and pulled him out.

The depth and size of wallows is often a testament to how heavily bull elk use them during the rut. For that reason alone, they are a key piece of sign that we need to be able to read. The fact that bulls sometimes get carried away with them is another lesson.

A good outfitter friend of mine, Billy Hoppe, tells the story of a group of people he took out on a horseback trip to do

some photography some years back. The trip took place in mid- to late August during the time when bulls are starting to use wallows heavily and are feeling the first strong urges of the rut.

The group was riding through elk country, going through the timber from one opening to another, and enjoying the whole scene when they ran into a piece of swampy ground. Billy knew horses can sink deeply in those swampy areas, so he was looking for a way around it when he spotted ahead of him what looked like a set of antlers sticking up out of the ground. That set of antlers turned out to be a bull elk that was in a wallow.

The wallow was a good-sized one—one that several elk had been using—and it had been worked so hard that the marsh grass around it was all dug up and the wallow itself was deep with mud. Unfortunately, this five-point bull had broken through a hard crust of marsh grass on the edge and become mired in that mud. Now, the bull was tired. He was sinking deeper. And he was profoundly stuck. As the group got off their horses and walked over, they could see that the mud was clear up to the bull's antlers. The bull was trying to pull himself up out of the mud with his front feet, but he just didn't have the strength. The men walked up so close to the elk that they were able to touch him on the nose, and the bull didn't even fight them. It was obviously a death struggle that the bull was losing.

Billy and the group formulated a plan to try to get the bull out of the wallow. Their plan was to take a lariat rope and run it around the antlers. Then they'd take both ends of the rope and dally it around the saddle horn of Billy's horse. Then, as the elk got up out of the wallow, Billy would let go of one end of the rope and it would slide out. It was a great plan. But it didn't work.

When the elk did lurch out of the wallow and when he did get his feet under him, he charged Billy's horse instead. For his part, the horse didn't want anything to do with that elk. And the rodeo began. So instead of dropping one end of the rope, Billy dropped both ends of the rope and tried to handle his horse instead. After a quick charge at the horse, the elk turned and took off with the lariat rope. Though the group followed the path the bull took in his escape, they never did find the rope. Those lariat ropes, once they get kinked, are pretty hard to get undone. So we figured that this rope would be dragged by the elk until one end of it hung up on something or the bull shed his antlers.

What surprised the group the most about the incident was

how quickly, and how strongly, that bull had come back to life once he came out of that mud. He had been completely submerged in that mud for some time. He appeared to be completely fatigued. Then he got that second surge of adrenaline and was up and gone. It's the same thing I've seen happen when hunters have tried tracking wounded elk. A wounded animal will go off and lie down and you think the hunt is over, but as soon as he sees the figure of a man coming toward him, his second burst of adrenaline is unbelievable and he can run for miles. A lot of people have lost their elk because of that second burst. With it, a bull elk can travel a long, long way before he lies down again.

Of course, if you were good enough at reading sign to get a shot into that bull elk in the first place, you should be good enough, too, at the long-distance tracking it takes to find him again. All it takes is the ability to follow tracks and to judge their age, with or without snow. There shouldn't be any elk at all that you can't find—just as long as you use some patience, some experience, and read the signs that the animals leave behind.

Chapter Two

CHAPTER THREE

When to Hunt

Old habits are powerful, powerful things, and all of us have established our hunting habits over the years. We tend to hunt in particular places. We hunt them in particular ways. We hunt them at particular times. We come back year after year and do the same things over and over again. While there is much to be said for knowledge, experience, and tradition in elk hunting, the truth of the matter is that sometimes we get into a rut. As a result, while we reap the benefits of all the good things about those habits, we are also doomed to repeat our own mistakes. And so it is with the quandary of when to hunt.

In the September archery season in Montana, for example, we are often blessed (or is it cursed?) with crisp, cool mornings, heat during the midday, and then cool temperatures returning at dusk. It's also a time of year that's blessed (or is it cursed?) with long days and short nights. As a result, most bowhunters have established a definite hunting routine.

ELK TACTICS

They rise in the pre-dawn darkness, hunt the first few hours of daylight in the cool temperatures, return to camp for a late breakfast and a long lounging period at midday, and then hunt the last few hours of the day until darkness.

In a way, that's a good plan. You get to hunt in all the cool hours. You get to lay up and relax in the heat of day. And you don't have to try to stay on your feet and hunt through what is often fourteen or fifteen hours of daylight.

The trouble is that we get fixed on this hunting habit. We seem to be cursed to repeat these things day after hunting day and year after hunting year. And I can't help but think that the elk know it, too—especially the pressured elk. They're on the lookout for hunters early in the morning. They know they're safe in their beds at midday. They're wary and push their evening activities until the brink of legal shooting time. They almost seem to know that the daylight is too long for a hunter to be out there all day. They seem to know that the nights are too short for a hunter to recharge his batteries with sleep before he has to awaken to hunt again.

So hunters repeat their old habits during the peak calling season for elk. They continue their practice of morning hunts and evening hunts and rarely vary the pattern. Hunters later in the year often have their patterns, too, though shorter days allow for more hours to sleep and fewer hours to hunt as the season wears on. But even then, we seem cursed to repeat our habits season after season.

The point of all this is that from what I've witnessed over the years—and the changes I've witnessed—I think it's time all of us re-think our old habits. It's time to sort them out, keeping the good and discarding the bad and looking at some new options along the way. There are some hunting opportunities being missed out there because we always do the same old thing. Or, at least, there are some possibilities that we should be thinking about. The question of when to hunt isn't as cut-and-dried as I first thought it to be. It's time to explore some new tactics as they relate to the old question of when to hunt.

If you sleep-in at elk camp, you'll miss some outstanding opportunities to catch an elk at the first light of morning.

Elk at Dawn

You won't find many slugabeds in a good elk hunting camp. The day starts early, sometimes long before the day is much more than a smear of light in the eastern sky. There's coffee, tea, or hot chocolate to be made. A hot drink with a couple of several-day-old donuts to dunk in it or a few packets of instant oatmeal in a big mug of boiling water constitutes breakfast in many do-it-yourself camps. Or, if you're lucky enough to have somebody to cook for you, maybe you'll have a big hot breakfast. But in any case, there's no lounging around the breakfast table when you're done. The elk are up and about already, and you've got a rendezvous planned with them somewhere up the mountain.

This daily routine of elk hunting often begins with a marathon hike or a horseback ride to beat the clock. In the process, you've got to beat the elk to a certain distant meadow or a point on a particular feeding path. If you tarry, you're out of luck. If you don't head off the herd, you're unlikely to ever catch up with them. If you oversleep, or are simply slow to crawl out of your sleeping bag, you might just as well stay in bed until noon.

Dawn is one of those times when just about every elk in

Chapter Three

ELK TACTICS

Hunters have to penetrate far enough, early enough, before the elk move out of the clearings toward their bedding areas.

the mountains is up on its feet and moving. It's chilly on those fall mornings—sometimes downright cold. But the elk seem to thrive on the cold mountain air. If it's breeding season, the bulls are bugling and chasing cows out in the meadows. Even if the breeding season is past, it's still your best shot to find a bull out in the open, grabbing a last mouthful of grass before heading to his bed for the day.

But if the first hour or two of shooting light is the best for finding active elk, it's also the most demanding on the hunter to put himself, or herself, into a position where he or she's within calling or shooting distance of a bull. I can't begin to tell you how many hours I've spent hiking on trails in the dark before dawn. It's sometimes foolish to remember just how dark it was, and how dark it remained for how long, just to reach some distant rendezvous with the elk.

I'm not the only one who has hit the trail at 3 A.M. or 4 A.M. or 5 A.M., just to be at a certain spot at first light. Some routinely ride horseback in the dark. Others hike the trails on foot. Still others take the motorized route to the top of the mountain, giving themselves plenty of time, after they park their rigs, to move on a little farther. I, myself, have even strapped a sleeping bag and pack to my back, hiked a long trail the afternoon before, then slept wherever sunset found me, just so—by daybreak—I'd be able to reach a distant park where I felt the elk of my dreams would find me.

Why do it? That's simple. It works. And it's just about a necessity. Somehow, some way, you've got to at least be able to meet the elk on their way back to their high country bedding areas. And, better yet, you should be in those places ahead of the elk, so that they can travel to you in the first hours after dawn.

If I were to pick my favorite spot to hunt on a mountain, it would be from about halfway to two-thirds of the way to the top. That has always been the most productive zone for me. That's where the best concentrations of elk tend to be.

And while I realize that elk will often feed down low and then follow trails to their beds farther up the slope, it seems like, by the time you catch up to those elk in the morning, it's halfway to two-thirds of the way up the slope. By the time legal shooting hours arrive, that's where they are.

This is one of the reasons why hunters who have horses to carry them always seem to have such a big leg-up on the competition. It's not necessarily that they're better hunters once the horse is tied or hobbled and the foot hunting begins. It's more a matter of the fact that they're able to make it so much farther, so much easier, so much faster, so much earlier. They're able to make that climb before dawn, leaving the bulk of the foot hunters in their wake, far back down the mountain.

One time we were on one of those early morning horseback rides far back into the mountains. We got up early that morning, the outfitter and I, and had taken a couple of hunters with us. The bulk of the ride was just what you'd expect in elk country during the hunting season. It was still dark. We were moving along. Eventually, we would go past where the foot hunters could reach.

If only we got back far enough, we could get ahead of elk that were moving out in front of the onslaught of foot hunters, too. This time, we found the elk by riding right into the middle of them. If we looked real close, through the darkness, we could just barely see the outlines of the elk. So we

Chapter Three

ELK TACTICS

opted to wait with them. We stopped the horses and just sat there. It was quiet. There were elk all around. It was just a matter of time until there was enough daylight so we could do something about it. But as we sat there, one of the hunters just couldn't sit still. He had a fanny pack on his saddle that had a zipper on it. Finally, he reached down and ran that zipper up to open up his fanny pack. That sound was all it took. It wasn't a sound of nature. And all of the elk in front of us spooked and left the area.

After all the riding in the darkness and making the rendezvous with the elk, one wrong sound had blown the whole situation. The shapes in the darkness hadn't disturbed them. The sounds of the horses walking didn't bother them either. But that one zipper made the whole group of elk leave. And we never found them again.

In this case, the elk had been silent so we could ride into them. Most often during the breeding season, the main case to be made for early morning hunts is the fact that the elk are bugling at that time of day. You can eliminate a whole bunch of country without elk, and pinpoint the areas where elk are holding, if you can hear the bulls bugling in the predawn darkness or in the first hour or two after sunrise.

Of course, you still have to hike to get into the area where you can hear those bugles. And you have to understand, too, that elk can be a bit cagey about where they hold at that time of year.

One of the realizations I've arrived at over years of observing hunters in my piece of elk country is that a lot of hunters miss the good areas completely. We get a few archers around here, but not a whole lot. And, for the most part, if they're not hunting with an outfitter or a guide, they usually end up hunting in the wrong spots. They'll hunt for a few days and figure there isn't anything around, then move out and try another area. A lot of times, elk in the rut will hole up in a relatively small area. In the timber, you have a hard time locating them, unless you get close enough to hear them.

I can remember one time when I was out trying to shoot

some videotape of elk during the rut. In this case, we had used the early morning to spot the elk, and we heard them bugling. By locating them that way, we had the rest of the day to try to work on them.

As it turned out, it wasn't until the early afternoon that we got into the right position. And the elk were still there. I worked my way up onto a little ridge and got ready. In turn, the elk started to get pretty vocal. It was obvious there was more than one bull out there, and the bulls were bugling back and forth to each other.

When big herd bulls do that, they normally will not leave their cows, except to chase a smaller satellite bull away from the herd. Then they'll go back. As a result, it's often frustrating when you try to lure the herd bull within camera range, or bow-and-arrow range for that matter. The satellite bulls, on the other hand, are pretty easy. They're on the move around the main herd anyway. If you call, you always stand a good chance of bringing one of them in. And just because they're satellite bulls doesn't mean they're necessarily small. Sometimes they're in the six-point category and are respectable bulls. They're just not as big as the big boy with the herd. Other satellites are smaller, three-, four-, or five-points.

On this occasion, we worked our way within about two hundred yards of where the elk were bugling. Our position there was perfect. There were open parks ahead of us, with a draw that meandered to another slope where there was a timbered hillside. The elk were on the other side of that timbered hillside.

Periodically, we could see elk moving around up there. What we didn't know was that there was a wallow between us and them. As the afternoon wore on, the younger satellite bulls were leaving the old herd bull and his cows and jumping into the wallow. We couldn't see the wallow, but we'd see them wander into an area clean and come out all muddy.

As soon as one bull came out of the wallow, I cow-called to him. The bull was almost solid with mud. But at the sound, he straight-lined right toward us. I figure that, in his mind, he thought maybe this was a lone cow that had split

Chapter Three

ELK TACTICS

Morning hunts are usually uphill affairs, trying to catch up to elk that are also moving up the mountain.

off from the herd and now would be his alone. In any event, the bull came in almost at a trot. Along the way, he'd have to drop down into the draw and we'd lose track of him for a time until he was almost on top of us. But he was an active bull. When he stopped, I'd cow-call again and he'd bugle. He'd get moving again, and then when he stopped, I'd cow-call again and he'd bugle.

If I had to figure the distances involved, the whole affair began with a distance of four hundred to five hundred yards between the elk and me. But all it took was three total cow calls before I had him very, very close. When the muddy, small six-point finally stepped up out of the draw and came to a stop, he was just ten yards away. And all I could see were his antlers. I cow-called to him one last time, and he stepped up the hill into full sight. How rutty was this bull?

Let's put it this way, his eyes were literally bugged out. They showed red around the edges. This bull was about as steamed up as you can get.

His focus was totally on me, but he couldn't quite understand what he was seeing. He was looking for a cow that wasn't there. Instead, there was this lump of something close to the ground. The bull started to make this ten-yard circle. I cow-called again, and the sound seemed to startle him. He heard elk. But he couldn't see elk. And it finally must have hit him that something was terribly wrong, because he jumped and ran out of there. It was all just too close.

What would have happened had I not cow-called that last time, I'm not sure. But ever since then, I've remembered not to call at them when they're that close and that focused on where the sound was coming from. Even if you call softly, it's going to ruin the situation. You're better off just staying quiet and letting the elk work out the details of where that cow he heard has disappeared to. If there was another lesson I learned, it's that spraying elk scent into the air and saturating the area with scent is also a good plan for these close encounters. Without it, all it would have taken is the wrong whiff of wind and that bull would have smelled me easily.

That the elk were so active in the middle of the day didn't really come as much of a surprise. I've had good hunting at midday before. And I've heard plenty of bugling and seen wallow activity during those midday hours, too.

But in this case, as in so many others, locating the elk came in the early morning. That early-morning locating set the stage for the hunting that followed for the rest of the day. When keying in on early-morning elk, hunters should remember that most elk will be following trails that lead them from their nocturnal feeding areas toward their bedding areas. Until or unless food sources change, or hunters force them into new patterns, these feeding trails will be the same morning after morning and will also be the same year after year, if you happen to be hunting during the same time period.

If you know where the feeding trails are, you can try to set yourself up to intercept the elk. Often the type of terrain

Chapter Three

and timber determines how quickly or slowly the elk move on those trails. If the terrain is open and the elk feel vulnerable in it, they'll often walk right through. If there's cover and there's no one pushing them, they'll often move more slowly. One of my hunting areas offers just the perfect mix. The elk feed down the slope in the evening. In the morning, they head back up. The area they pass through offers good cover, but not a lot of deadfall. There's some food in there. But it's not wide open.

As a result, the elk seem to fan out as they move up toward their beds. Instead of moving steadily, they sort of feed themselves in the direction they want to go. If I can reach the spot early enough in the morning, that's the perfect situation. The elk won't be there yet, and they can feed their way to me. If I choose to call them, I'm pulling them in a direction they already want to go. That's ideal. Of course, you don't always get there ahead of the elk. Sometimes, if they have already gone through, you have to try to catch up to them. It can be done. But it isn't easy and is far from a sure thing. Even an elk feeding slowly can move up a slope more easily than most hunters. Other times, you arrive at the same time as the elk. In this case, if they spot you before you spot them, you've bumped them and they'll make a quick exit from the area.

One time, I was filming elk there and had taken my dog along with me. The situation actually turned out better than you might think. I got there ahead of the elk. I did some calling. A bunch of cows came in. But rather than the dog scaring the elk, they seemed more curious than frightened. When they saw the dog, they got really inquisitive and came in pretty close.

I tried to repeat the situation again another year, but I got a late start. I just got in on the tail end of the herd and bumped them. When they saw me, they just took off. The end result was two hours of early-morning hiking and no film to show for it.

Your own success in hunting these little strips of timber on the feeding trails will be just as good, or perhaps just as bad. Your luck will improve on the days when the elk are a little late moving out of the feeding areas. If they move early, you're generally sunk. You can improve your luck, too, by planning to intercept the elk farther along on the trail. Sometimes it takes elk until 8, 9, or even 10 A.M. before they reach their bedding areas. The farther along on the trail you make your rendezvous, the better your chance of getting to the spot ahead of them.

Another thing you should be aware of as you plan your early morning rendezvous with elk is that elk tend to be where you find them. They aren't always in places where you plan them to be. You have to be ready for them any time. And you have to be able to identify them when you do come into contact with them.

One of the funnier elk stories I've heard turned out to be a bit of a joke on Billy Hoppe, of all people. Billy and I hunt a lot together. Billy grew up in the Gardiner area and is carrying on the family tradition as an outfitter there. He takes hunters out in the September bow season, through the general rifle season of October and November, and then in the special late season that runs into February.

If there's anybody around here that knows elk, it's Billy. He literally lives around elk and has lived around elk all his life. And he loves to call them, too.

In this case, Billy was breaking in a new guide for the fall hunting season. It was still early in the bow season, and each of them had a hunter he was doing calling for. It came to pass that they were in the same area and Billy heard his new guide trying to call elk. In private later, he told the guide, "Geez, you have to get a different elk call. You sound just lousy and that call is just crap. It sounds more like a crow than an elk. It's got a real tinny sound to it." That night, Billy called me and asked me if I could get a Power Bugle for him. I told him I'd even deliver one. So I set up a Power Bugle and got the bands all set, tested it, and got it to him so he could use it the following morning.

Billy, his guide, and the hunters started out on horseback in the dark the following morning. They were following a long path that required almost two hours of riding before

Chapter Three

ELK TACTICS

they reached the area where they expected to find the elk. Along the way, Billy gives the Power Bugle to the guide, saying, "I'll show you how to blow this thing and you practice it as we go along the trail." As the group rode along, the guide started practicing. He asked Billy how he was doing. Billy said he was doing better.

The group was still about a mile from where they wanted to be to begin hunting the elk, and it was just starting to break daylight. The guide blew his call again. But this time, an elk answered nearby. But Billy, thinking it was still his guide, says, "Now that one, you did really good. You're getting the hang of it. You're sounding like an elk." The guide told him, "That wasn't me. That was an elk."

The guide and his hunter got off their horses right there and headed up the slope. They made a big circle and got above where they figured the bull would be. And the guide made just one squeal on that new call. That was all it took. The bull came in at full-speed and stopped just ten steps away. The hunter bagged the elk. It was all over. It was just that easy. And everyone laughed about it afterwards, about how good that last bugle sounded and how the guide really got the hang of it on that early-morning ride.

As we all well know, it doesn't always work out that way. Not all bull elk are that active, either. But it's a testament to early-morning hunts that elk are often more active, and more elk are up on their feet, at that time than at any other time of day.

If you can blast yourself out of bed early enough, if you have a way to get yourself back in far enough, and if you key in on the feeding routes that elk will be following at that time of day, you have a good plan for locating elk. Once those elk are located, you can figure out exactly what you want to do with them. You can hunt them on the spot. You can wait and hunt them later. You have the rest of the day ahead of you to execute your hunting plans.

There are other times of the day that may be as good for hunting elk. But there's no better time to locate elk than early in the morning. And you just might bag a bull then, too.

Bulls are often in the mood to start bugling again after a few hours of napping in the morning.

Chapter Three

The Neglected Noon Hunt

The middle of the day has never been the favorite time for most elk hunters. Elk are thought to be in their beds, snoozing. They're hiding somewhere in the deepest, darkest pockets of black timber. They're thought to be totally inactive. A fair number of hunters are snoozing, too, as they rest up between hunts in the morning and hunts in the evening. As a result, the noon hunt has been the neglected hunt for most who seek elk.

But my experiences with hunting at midday have not been this way. In fact, sometimes they have offered excellent opportunities to call elk, shoot elk, and photograph elk. And if I had a crystal ball that really looked into the future, I'd tell you for certain that the hunt at midday will only get better in the years to come.

It isn't just my experiences with hunting in the middle of the day that make me say this. It's also a reasonable, logical, explainable phenomenon as well. Think about it. Elk are often active all night long, especially during the breeding season when bulls are chasing cows and defending harems from other bulls. They're active at first light, too, as they leave the feeding grounds and head toward their bedding areas. Then, for a time, everything settles down. Elk are tired. They lounge in their beds. They sleep. And, as a result, many elk hunters leave the forests to the elk. The hunters head back to camp for that second breakfast. They may take a nap, too. Often, the hunters leave the hunting areas alone until the sun gets low in the afternoon sky, when they return to make an evening hunt. That's when the elk are up on their feet and moving again, looking for some mouthfuls of grass as they work out into clearings and eventually head back to their feeding areas.

It has been my experience, however, that the elk aren't necessarily quiet all day long, especially during the breeding season. They may go quiet and sleep for a couple of hours after they move into their bedding areas. But after that sleep, they either make themselves more active, or they can be convinced to become active by an elk caller. The location of their activity may be different than during early morning and evening. The activity may be limited to the immediate vicinity of the bedding area. But they do come alive again.

Perhaps the best story about this again has to do with my good friend Billy Hoppe. Billy has been around elk long enough and often enough himself, and we've worked midday elk together often enough, that he probably takes advantage of midday elk more than most people. And the hunters he guides have definitely benefited from it.

When you listen to bugling elk in the middle of the day, they may be calling back to you from their beds.

Chapter Three

ELK TACTICS

Billy was guiding a bowhunter in the mountains near Gardiner, and they had been following an elk herd all morning long. They had spotted the herd early. But they couldn't quite catch up to them. As the herd worked toward its bedding area, Billy and the bull in the bunch had been bugling back and forth. As is often the case, however, when you're trailing elk moving out ahead of you, Billy just couldn't seem to get the bull to come back toward him.

Finally, the elk moved into a place that Billy recognized as a prime bedding area. It was just the type of spot the elk would be looking for. It was the type of spot where they'd bed and rest after being on their feet much of the night and the first hours of the day. Rather than charging in and bumping them from the bedding area, Billy did the next best thing. He decided to catch a nap, too. He turned to his hunter and told him, "We're going to let those elk lie down and sleep and we're going to do the same thing." I'm sure the hunter could hardly believe what he was being told. Here they were, within perhaps two hundred yards of where the elk were bedded down. The hunter had paid Billy good money to hunt. And now his guide was telling him not to hunt elk, but to take a nap instead. It must have taken unbelievable faith in Billy for the hunter to agree to what his guide asked. But he did agree.

In truth, it was a great situation for a nap. It was a beautiful day. There was no wind. The temperature was perfect. So Billy and his hunter took a long nap. About three hours later, Billy told the hunter it was time to get ready. The pair made a circle around the bedding area so they could take a position above it, again about two hundred yards from where they felt the elk would be. Billy led off with a cow sound, and then a bugle. Immediately, the bull answered. It took almost no time at all for the bull to cover the two hundred yards. The bull came strongly up the slope. And the hunter put an arrow into him at sixteen paces and the hunt was over.

Billy had played the bull just right. He had bedded the elk down and given them some time. He waited for some hours to pass for the animals to digest their food, to catch a nap, and to become receptive to coming in. Rather than tromp around during that time looking for other elk that may or may not have been in the area, Billy and his hunter had simply rested themselves. When the time was right, they worked into a good calling position, made a good setup, and bagged themselves a bull.

If the hunter hadn't had complete faith in his outfitter, the end result would undoubtedly have been different. The hunter could have told Billy that there was no way he was going to nap his hunt away. They were going to find elk and hunt elk. But had that happened, the hunter never would have gotten the bull he got. Billy had the situation analyzed perfectly. He located the elk, got into position above him, worked him, and brought him in. In retrospect, that sounds so easy. But Billy's knowledge and the hunter's faith in that knowledge made it all work.

The difference between elk at dawn and a midday hunt is very much a matter of locating the elk. Locating elk at first light or in the first hours of daylight is relatively easy. They're up on their feet and moving. Their movements are also pretty predictable, usually a matter of moving from feeding areas to bedding areas. Locating elk at midday is more difficult. They aren't on the move. They're holding in one tight spot, or perhaps in a small general area. And even if they're up on their feet and bugling, the sounds of those bugles are more difficult to hear. Perhaps that's because it's more likely to be windy at midday and wind muffles the sounds. Maybe it's because the air being heated by the sun and the rising air currents of the mountains carry the sounds away. Or it could simply be that much of the midday bugling is done in areas with timber, rather than open meadows. Whatever the reason, locating the elk is more difficult. But once you locate the elk, the action can actually be quicker than calling early in the morning or late in the evening. Early and late in the day, the elk's minds are primarily on food, water, or bed. In the middle of the day, those thoughts aren't at the forefront of their minds.

How fast can elk respond to midday calling? Once an elk makes up its mind to come in, it takes just about the same

Chapter Three

ELK TACTICS

If you can work into the right calling position, often all it takes is one or two calls and the elk are on their way straight in.

amount of time as it takes to read this sentence. I can remember one time when Gordon Eastman and I were filming and hunting elk. It was at midday, and we were sitting down and taking a break when we heard a sound. Gordon said the sound was a bird. I said it was an elk. I got out my cow call and called back. I waited a few minutes, then cow-called again and got a call in return. Before Gordon could even set up his camera, a cow elk ran up to within fifteen yards of us. We were spotted. We couldn't move. Gordon never did get any footage of that elk before she wandered off.

Another time, I was hunting with a different friend and

working my way along a ridge, stopping every few hundred yards to call. One of those calls got a quick response from just up the slope, followed by the sound of pounding hoofbeats. Before I could even get my face mask pulled down, a lone cow ran down at full speed and came to a sudden stop twenty-five yards away. Then she whirled and ran back to where she came from just as fast. The whole incident was started, executed, and completed in twenty seconds or less.

That type of response is common with elk at midday, especially if you have a cow elk that's lost track of the rest of the herd. That cow is by herself, and she must be looking for some company. When she hears an elk sound, she comes in a hurry. And, as I found out, when she doesn't find what she wants, she can leave in a hurry, too.

One tactic to make the most of a midday hunt is to create a situation just like Billy did. You first need to locate a bedding area. Then you have to figure out a way to get a position somewhere on the slopes above it.

The best calling position for elk and almost every other species I've ever tried to work has always been from above. Being on the same level with them can be effective, too. Trying to call them from below is by far the least desirable position of all. Trying to figure out why animals are more willing to come upslope to a caller, rather than downslope, would all be a matter of conjecture. In truth, I don't have any idea. All I know is that animals would rather come up.

Another rule of thumb when getting into position to call midday elk is to remember that all nearby elk may not be in the same closely confined area. There have been a lot of times when I've been in areas where elk were bedded down and I've jumped a bull, he's taken off, and I figured I was done. I had ruined the area. But surprisingly—surprisingly to me anyway—there have been many times when that first bull was not alone. Especially in breeding season situations, but at other times of the year, too, elk will spread out a bit when they bed down. I've found other bulls anywhere from a handful of yards, to as many as two hundred yards, away from the first bull I jumped. If the second bull is a distance away, he might not get too excited about the first bull's

Chapter Three

hasty departure. As long as the first bull didn't run right past him and sweep him up in his wake, the other bull may still be there. If you're confident you're in a good position, call anyway. See and hear what responds. And don't be too shocked if another bull bugles back or comes in, or even if the first bull returns to the sounds of your call. A lot of bulls that weren't too badly bumped have returned to investigate the sounds that appear to be from another elk.

That strategy targets elk that you don't hear first, but that you suspect are in an area. But if you get close to the bedding area at midday, you'll often find that elk are bugling. Sometimes it may be just one elk. Other times, there could be a relative bugling frenzy going on. Sometimes you can start the frenzy yourself.

If you have a group of elk that are scattered throughout an area at midday—a bull here, some cows there, some brush bulls scattered in various areas—sometimes all it takes is an elk caller to get them all talking. I've had it happen when I heard just one bugle and set up to bugle back. That one exchange turned into some aggressive bugling between me and the bull, and pretty soon, you have other bulls chiming in. As is typical, you may not get the herd bull worked up enough to come to your calling. But those satellite bulls—some of which can be some very nice six-points—will come in. You get them all fired up. You get them talking. You bring them in. And one of the best times to do it is from late in the morning until early in the afternoon.

A prime example is a time when I went out to get some elk sounds. I was just going to record them. I didn't even have my bow along. From a humble start with just one elk answering, the bugling grew to the point that I had bulls on all sides of me. After getting the bulls started, I quit calling. I didn't have to call anymore. The bulls were firing each other up all by themselves. They didn't need me. The bugling went on for more than an hour before it finally stopped. When it did stop, it stopped cold. Something must have spooked the elk because the whole mountainside went quiet. But it had been quite a lively time up to that point.

And how all the bulls scattered through that area knew it was time to stop cold, I really don't know. But something made them go quiet all at once.

Another thing you should remember about midday calling is that it's a time when you can't always tell by the sound of a bull how big he might be. Judging the size of a bull by the sound he's making is always an unscientific judgment. Big bulls can sound squeaky. They might sound deep and hollow. Sometimes the biggest of bulls will be sore-throated from so much bugling on previous days and sound the worst. But what complicates matters at midday is that often the bulls aren't even on their feet. They're trying to bugle from a lying-down position as they rest in their beds. I've watched them try to do it. They'll throw their head back and try to get the same sounds as if they were on their feet. But they just can't do it. So don't judge too quickly by sounds, especially at midday.

You need to remember, too, that when you hunt midday elk, you're definitely hunting them in terrain that is very much to the elk's choosing. The areas near bedding areas are almost always timbered. At best, you may have small openings. You may have some thinner timber that you're working. But, for the most part, you're tackling elk that are in country that offers the most security for them.

Elk that are holding in these areas also tend to be lying down, at least at the start. And cows and calves will often remain bedded, even if the herd bull or satellite bulls are up on their feet. As a result, you've got to enter these areas carefully and keep your eyes wide open at all times. If not, you may ruin a good calling situation by alerting cows and calves.

I can remember one hunt I was on with Keith Wheat, a good hunting friend from a number of years ago, when we heard some bulls bugling late in the morning. We were archery hunting at the time, and we could tell that there were several bulls and a number of cows and calves in this one drainage.

The terrain held scattered trees. The bulls were up on their feet and moving some. It was a good chance to try to move in on them and get in on the action. One of the bulls

Chapter Three

eventually worked his way to the far side of the drainage. At least one more bull was holding on the near side. So Keith and I decided to split up. He'd take the far side bull. I was going to work the one on the near side.

My bull was somewhere below me in the timber, and he was bugling often. As I worked my way down the slope, I'd bugle back periodically. I was working closer and closer. I knew I was getting very close. I knew I had better drop down to my hands and knees if I was going to get any closer.

Hunting from a hands-and-knees position isn't easy. You can't move very quickly. From that low viewpoint, you also can't see very well. But I had to do it. If I stayed upright, I knew I was getting close enough that the bull would see me. The cover was too thin to hide me. I'd have to make the best of it.

I crawled that way for about one hundred yards and knew the bull was about seventy yards in front of me. He was close, but still not near close enough for a shot. I had him pinpointed. I'd just keep crawling along.

When I got to that position, I tried to peer ahead and spot the bull. But I had my camouflage net down and I couldn't see very well. All the crawling had worked up a bit of a sweat, too, and my glasses had steamed up on me. So I slowly raised my hand up and lifted the head net up so I could let in some fresh air to defog the glasses. I waited there for quite a while to let my glasses defog, but they still weren't clear. Finally, I tried to get my handkerchief out so I could wipe the glasses clean. But as I did that, I looked to my right and there were twenty head of cows looking at me. When I turned my head to look at them, they all barked. When they barked, they took off. And, of course, the bull blew out of there, too.

It was a classic case of midday hunting with elk scattered throughout an area. I had known where the bull was because he was sounding off. But I didn't have a clue about where the cows were. And eventually those cows—with a little help from my foggy glasses—ruined the whole situa-

Bull elk will tear up the ground as they work up wallows or create a display area.

tion. Since then, I've always remembered that when you're working a herd bull, you never know how many eyes you have looking at you. And it's often the elk you don't see that will get you.

I tried to follow the band of elk. They went for about a mile and half into a high mountain basin, went into the timber, and never came out. They knew I was behind them, and the chances of me ever working up on them in there were slim. So my hunt was over.

For his part, Keith knew which direction his elk were moving, and he got ahead of them and set up. The herd all came past him, and he could have killed a spike or several cows, but the bigger bull was out just a little far for a shot. He tried to follow his elk, too, but he never saw them again. His key to getting on that herd of elk in the first place was to know where they were going and to get ahead of them. Once they got past him, his chances of catching up to them

ELK TACTICS

again were slim. So his hunt was over, too.

Stalking your way into an elk bedding ground doesn't always end in a failure to get a shot. And it doesn't mean that you won't get a shot, either, just because you have other elk bedded down that you don't see right away. One time, I was hunting with Murphy Love, and we followed a bull for four hours. He paralleled the side of a mountain, holding about the same elevation, but we just couldn't seem to get closer to him, even though he'd answer our bugles periodically. When he finally went quiet for good, we knew he had bedded down. We worked our way very slowly, glassing a lot, and quit calling completely. Finally, Murphy spotted his antlers. The bull was bedded down on a little knoll below us. What we didn't know was that his cows were bedded at the same elevation we were at, and even above us. We had worked our way right into the middle of them.

When we spotted the bull's antlers, Murphy made a cow sound and the bull instantly bugled back to him. After a bit, Murphy cow-called again and the bull got up and started coming up the slope. Unfortunately, the bull ran into a deadfall tree and hung up there. He stayed behind that tree for the longest time, looking for the cow he had heard. It seemed like an eternity. Murphy finally cow-called again, and the bull worked his way around that big, deadfall tree. When he got around the end of it, he came up the hill a little bit and was just one hundred yards away. When the bull stopped again, Murphy called and here he came. The bull came within twenty-five yards and turned broadside, to go above us. When he stopped for an instant, Murphy took a shot at him with his bow. Unfortunately again, the arrow went beneath the bull and disintegrated when it smacked a rock beyond the elk. The bull jumped up the hill about five yards. Unfortunately, once again, Murphy, in his disgust, expressed his disgust out loud. When the elk heard that voice, all the cow calling that Murphy did thereafter had no effect in bringing that bull back in close again. All the cows that had been with the bull came in, responding to the calling. But the bull never came back and Murphy never got another shot.

Working on midday elk is always a bit of a gamble. You have to know where the elk are bedding to start with. You have to get close enough to call and lure them out of these areas or to get them fired up enough with their bugling that they wander out by themselves. But you also know that if you blow them out of the bedding areas and scare them, they may travel for miles before they stop and your chances of ever catching up to them are slim.

But I still like the midday hunt. It has been a most effective time for me to call elk. Unless a whole bunch of hunters change their habits, I expect it to continue to be effective. Right now, there simply aren't that many hunters who are going after elk at that time of day, even though overall hunting pressure on elk has increased. As long as those other hunters choose to stay in camp at midday or to lay up and rest somewhere back in the mountains, the midday hunt will continue to be a good alternative and may actually get better.

As hunting pressure increases in the early morning and late evening, the elk will respond to it and become less responsive. If they're left alone at midday, they'll begin to respond at that time even more. It's no secret that elk are always the easiest to work when the pressure is least. And, for the most part, there are only a few of us hunting and calling elk at the neglected hour of noon.

The Evening Hunt

Evening hunts in elk country are almost too good to be true. It's not that they're more productive than morning hunts or that the elk are more responsive than they can be at midday. No, it's more a matter of evening in elk country itself.

Some of my fondest memories of evening hunts have nothing to do with the animals I saw or the elk I've taken. Instead, it's the memories of the evenings themselves. I can remember the night I sat on a high ridge and watched people less fortunate than me below. It's a memory I'll never forget. The hunt itself had been a good one, though I cut it short before sending an arrow at an elk. That night,

Chapter Three

ELK TACTICS

In the evening, elk are back on their feet again, often coming back down the mountain slopes toward feeding areas.

it didn't seem to matter.

I had located a group of elk rousing from their beds just as the sun was ready to set. I could hear the calves talking to their mothers. I could hear the mothers talking back. A few squeals let me know that there was at least one bull in the bunch with them. This was back in the days before cow calls became a regular part of my arsenal. And the bull didn't seem to want to leave the group and respond to my intermittent bugles.

So I worked my way within about 150 yards of the herd and planned to ambush them as they moved down the slope toward their feeding area. It was a good plan. But it wasn't good enough. The elk talked back and forth in their bedding area for nearly an hour, but they just wouldn't leave it. As the sun set and the shadows started to darken in the timber where I waited, the elk talk went on and on. Finally, the elk started to move—slowly. They worked a few yards down the slope, stopped, and talked some more. I waited. And waited some more. I watched the trail I knew they'd follow, but no elk appeared. And it kept getting darker.

It wasn't until the day was just about gone for good that

the first cow appeared on the trail. She was walking slowly, tentatively, and eventually came to within twenty-five yards of where I lay in wait. When she appeared, I brought up my bow and tried to look through the sights. But there just wasn't enough light left. Not even at twenty-five yards could I have made a certain shot. So I waited for that cow to move behind some brush and I slowly and quietly backed out of the ambush.

I moved back far enough that the other elk wouldn't see me. And I sat there for a time, listening to the sound of the elk parade moving down the slope. They were talking all the way. I never did know how many elk were in the bunch. The bull, or bulls, weren't vocal enough for me to get a fix on how many of them there might have been with the herd. There was no point in trying to get a look and thereby blowing them out of the country. I was going to be hunting that area for the next few days, and I had their bedding area located.

As I hiked my way down the ridge that evening, hustling to make it out before total darkness hid my trail, I looked into the valley below. While I was up here with the elk, the people down there were going through their workaday lives, the lights of their homes and towns and cars marking the places they were going and where they had been. In that cool mountain evening, I had to count my blessings. Up here in elk country, life was good. I'd had a close encounter with one of the grandest big game animals of them all. And if I was going home without an arrow in one, that was fine, too. It just gave me an excuse to come back tomorrow and spend more time with them.

Evenings in the mountains are like that. They are beautiful times. But the windows of opportunity they offer to bowhunters can be narrow ones indeed.

Just as that experience with elk was decided by a few scant minutes of failing daylight, many evening hunts are determined by elk being just a bit ahead of schedule or a bit behind it. The more pressure the elk are feeling, the smaller the margin for error. The less pressure the elk are feeling, the wider the window of opportunity opens.

Chapter Three

ELK TACTICS

To understand the why's, where's, and when's of hunting in the evening, you have to understand the lifestyle of the elk. We all know that mountain elk generally move up the slope toward bedding areas in the morning. They stay up there, in or near bedding areas, all day. Then, in the evening, they emerge and feed again, working toward the feeding areas where they'll generally spend the night.

The timing of that emergence from bedding areas and the move back down the mountain can be influenced by several things. If the weather has been hot, the elk might wait until the cool of the evening before they move. If the hunting pressure is on, they tend to move later and later. If there is decent grass in little meadows near the beds, they might spend considerable time there before hitting the feeding trail for good. All these factors can affect the success of locating and moving in on elk late in the day.

One of the tactics to increase the window of opportunity in the evening is to hunt elk in meadows close to their feeding areas. That generally means hunting them at fairly high elevations. If you're a foot hunter, that elevation often means you're hunting them far from your camp or far from your vehicle. That means a hike out in the dark. But sometimes, that's the best strategy.

In elk country, most hunters are still day hunters. Offhand, if I had to guess, I'd say 95 percent of the resident hunters in most states fall into that category. They don't take a week or two off. They hunt one or two days. They pick a drainage for the day's hunt. They walk up a ridge or the creek bottom. Then they turn around and head out.

There's nothing wrong with this. But often that return trip is thought to be just the journey home. After going through the country once, they figure that nothing is behind them. So they're more intent on covering ground on the return trip than they are in hunting it. That's a major mistake. And it pretty much eliminates the evening hunt.

Instead, any hunter would be well advised to hunt the way back as hard as he or she hunted the way in. For one thing, you've put yourself in a better position than you were in at the start of the day. You've gained the elevation. You're hunting down on the elk. You're in a better position to see elk and to call elk, just because you're hunting down.

There are other factors that come into play here, too. A lot of times, the game is at a lower elevation than you think it is. Back in the days when I was an inveterate bighorn sheep hunter, I kept telling myself that my motto would be "Hunt low. And hunt slow." That means stay off the mountain tops. It means hunt the middle of the mountain. And when you're hunting—hunt! And hunt slowly. Over the years, when I'd follow that motto, I'd find game. As I've gotten older, I don't have to tell myself that so much anymore. When you're young, you want to cover a lot of ground and hike to the top of the mountain and see what you can see. As you get older, nature has a way of slowing you down a bit. But it's still good advice for anyone who hunts his or her way back down the mountains on an evening hunt.

Another tactic to consider is to plan to stay somewhere on the mountain, closer to where the elk are active. Vince Yannone, a hunting friend of mine from the Helena area, always made it a practice to pack his bed on his back. He'd take his hunting pack, some food, and a sleeping bag with him. He'd plan to spend the night wherever night found him. Rather than make a one-day hunt of it, that allowed him to hunt the whole weekend. And it also gave him the latitude to stay in good elk country for a longer period of time.

If the weather is going to be fairly nice, a sleeping bag is just about all you need. If you're going to stay out longer, perhaps more of a spike camp would be in order. Take along a sleeping bag, a small tent, and perhaps a pack stove to allow you to eat hot meals. In either case, you can stay up the slopes in an area where the elk are likely to be more active earlier in the evening, instead of having to head for home just when, or just before, the elk start their evening feeding.

Exactly how far back in the mountains these areas might be depends a lot on hunting pressure. In areas that are hit hard by hunters, you often won't see the elk appear on the open slopes until just before the end of legal shooting. And

ELK TACTICS

sometimes, they don't come out until after that. In these areas of heavy pressure, the elk are also going to be more call-shy. If you can find an area with light pressure, or no pressure at all except you, you'll find the elk out in the

In the evening, hunters are often battling waning daylight as they try to lure an elk in before the shooting day ends.

openings much earlier. To locate them, just find a good vantage point and scan the openings with your binoculars. Elk in these areas also tend to be more vocal, beginning their bugling earlier in the evening, often early enough for you to work in close, call to them, and bring them in for a shot.

Those light pressure areas, of course, are the ones you always hope to find. Anytime you get an area with unwary elk, your chances of calling to them and bringing them in skyrocket. But even unwary elk may not respond quickly during the evening hunt. Remember, they've got feeding on their minds first and foremost.

As an example, there was the time when I was hunting and Gordon Eastman was filming. We were on our way toward putting together an elk hunting video, and we really wanted to get some good hunting footage on camera. It was late in the afternoon when we got into a position where we could call and where we thought the elk would be.

The elk were holding on another hillside when we started to call to them. And though the bull answered back to us, he just didn't sound that interested. He was responding just spasmodically to our bugles. He sounded far, far away. We were in a late-day situation where it would have been easy to pull out of there and move on. It sounded like the bull was going to stick with his cows on that distant hillside. He just wouldn't come in to us.

As Gordon and I discussed the situation, we began thinking that perhaps the best thing to do would be to pull out and come back the next morning. From his sounds, the bull was a good one. He was definitely worth putting on film. If we didn't spook him when we pulled out, he very likely would be somewhere in that area on the following day and perhaps he'd be more responsive to our calling.

We finally decided to stay where we were until dark, then sneak out of there as quietly as we could. As we were sitting there, I kept cow-calling and bugling periodically. It got to be dusk, and Gordon gave me the high sign to leave. By that time, I had spotted the bull, and he was only two hundred to three hundred yards away from us. I could see him. He wasn't moving out. The reason the sound was getting

Chapter Three

ELK TACTICS

fainter and why it sounded like he was moving out was because he wasn't always bugling right at us. He was bugling in the other direction. He was bugling at his cows.

Rather than leave, we kept cow-calling. I went back to my original position, and we waited him out. I was afraid that, if we packed up and moved, we'd spook him out of there. As it turned out, the bull really was more interested in us than we imagined. We called the elk right down to us. Some cows came in first. They meandered around a little open park that was right in front of us. The cows would talk to us once in a while. The rest of the time they were silent and feeding. Eventually, the bull came down, too. And he kept coming. And coming. The bull finally came to a stop just fifteen yards in front of Gordon.

The lesson I remember best about the situation was how long it took. It took a very, very long time. The whole scene I just described to you took place over a two-hour period, the last two hours of daylight on that mountain. Had we gone with our first thoughts, to just pull out of there, we probably never would have had the opportunity to call that bull in. We just stayed with the elk and worked them and worked them. Patience was the real key to it. We didn't overcall, but we called just enough to keep his interest up and eventually he responded.

Another lesson was that sounds can sometimes fool you badly. When an elk bugles in a different direction, he sounds like he's going away. You really have to take that into account when you're listening. You've got to use your best judgment. In this case, I could finally see him and see what was happening. Had I not seen him, we probably never would have stuck with it that long.

If you know the areas where elk are likely to feed in the evening, taking a stand and waiting them out is a popular strategy for rifle hunters. With the added range that a rifle provides, you don't have to wait quite so long for a bull to work in close. Just as long as you can catch them out in a clearing or even spot them from a distance and work in close enough for a long shot, you stand a good

Aside from actually shooting an elk in the evening, hunters can sometimes get a line on herds of elk to work the following day.

chance of bagging an evening bull.

In the heavily hunted Missouri Breaks of north-central Montana, taking a stand in the evening is a popular tactic, too. There, hunters are working elk that spend their days in the thick willows of a river bottom, working out into small clearings to feed in the last light of day. Hunters will take their stands—both on the ground and in the trees—and let the quiet of the river bottom settle in around them. As dusk falls, you can hear the cows and calves talking as they get up from their beds. You can hear the crunch of elk pushing their way through the willows. And if you've scouted well and know their patterns, you can set up an ambush.

As the hunting pressure gets heavier, the elk tend to move later and later. They become less and less responsive to calls, to the point that it's almost better not to use them at all. You just wait and hope they work out into the clearing you're watching before darkness.

Up in those tree stands, evening on the river is a joy to the senses all the while you wait. You see the last flights of geese of the day, winging their way up or down the river. You see the first owls of the evening as they search for their

ELK TACTICS

nocturnal prey. You hear the coyotes tune up and spread their songs across the whole scene. If you're absolutely quiet and patient and you plan your ambush well, you stand a chance of taking a big bowhunting prize as well. In no way should the chance be termed a good one with elk that are as spooky as they tend to be in the Breaks. But it is a chance. And each year some bowhunters cash in on taking a stand for elk in the evening.

I can still remember the evening when, after hunting on a distant island, Art Hobart and I were riding in his big jet boat back up the Missouri, heading for camp. As his spotlight pierced the darkness ahead, we caught the motion of a bowhunter waving his hand at us from a smaller boat, also working its way up against the current. As Art cut the motor, we could hear the man holler, "No wake. No waves." As we got closer, we could see why. There were three hunters in the boat with a big elk in there with them. The weight of the load had the water level up perilously close to the top of the gunwales. Any wave at all would have washed into the boat and the three men would have been swimming in the dark.

Later, at the landing, we helped the hunters tie up their boat and haul a big bull out of the boat and up onto the bank. The bull was in the 340 class, a fine six-point, and one of the men had shot it in the waning minutes of daylight. The three bowhunters then muscled the elk to the riverbank and into the boat, then climbed in themselves. They were pushing their luck taking that load back up the river. The body size of that elk was huge. It was much too heavy a load for the boat to handle, along with the weight of the men. Had Art and I not seen the man waving his hand up ahead of us, our wake most certainly would have swamped them. And we weren't the only ones out on the river that night either.

But the bowhunter from a distant state was all smiles at the landing. He had planned a strategy, and it had paid off. He was going home with the bowhunting elk of a lifetime. He had every reason to be smiling.

In much of elk country, even if elk like that aren't taken in the evening, the evening hunt provides a chance to locate elk that can be worked the following day. Bedding areas can be pinpointed. Feeding routes can be located. Elk are up on their feet again, providing hunters with a better opportunity to spot them.

And though the window of opportunity to take an elk is a relatively narrow one at that time of day, there is an opening. It may mean some hiking—or boating—in the dark. It may mean just one fleeting chance in the last shooting light of the day. It may mean developing a strategy that can help you another day. But evening hunts are the kind that you will remember well in the days, weeks, and years that follow for the spectacular scenes and remarkable experiences that are so much a part of them. Evening in elk country is a magical time, if only you take the time to hunt it, hunt it with patience, hunt it slowly, and hunt it well.

Chapter Three

CHAPTER FOUR

How to Hunt

There's something special about a wise old elk hunter. You can read it in his eyes. You can see it in his stride on a mountain trail. You can feel it in his every action—the way he scans the countryside, where he goes, what he does, how he conducts himself in elk country. Before he ever chambers a round in his rifle, or nocks an arrow on his bowstring, that hunter already has his elk. And he knows it. It's just a matter of where and when and how it's going to happen. But happen it will. His tag will be filled. With wise old elk hunters, it's a matter of experience and quiet confidence. No bragging or boasting is necessary. The hunter has been there before. He knows the elk and what they do. He knows the place they live. He knows that, somewhere down the trail, there's a bull elk waiting with his name on it. He just has to walk that trail.

Becoming this type of elk hunter isn't something that comes right away. It takes time and commitment to the elk-hunting game. It takes paying some dues before the season and during the season. And, usually, it takes many such seasons before you get really good at elk hunting.

The reason is that the start of this kind of confidence comes with success. Success begins with putting the right ingredients together—the scouting, the knowledge of the animal, the where to hunt and when to hunt. If you add the ingredient of how to hunt, and if you repeat the success often enough, the confidence grows. By that time, there isn't much luck involved anymore. The hunter knows how to read the country, how to put himself in just the right position at just the right time so that luck naturally comes his way.

A lot of elk hunters, especially elk hunters early in their careers, just don't understand this. They don't realize the importance of putting themselves in a position for success. They don't understand the planning that goes into it. They don't realize the investment that an old elk hunter has put into the game. Novice elk hunters look past the importance of the setup in hopes of finding success without it. They bank their fortunes on lucking into the right spot at the right time. In the process, every elk becomes a problem elk, not just the pressured elk that pose problems for even veteran hunters.

Elk hunting is a matter of investment, banking the time and the experiences necessary to learn how to hunt. Either you make that investment yourself. Or you pay big dollars to an outfitter or guide who has made that investment for you. Either way, it's a price that has to be paid to become consistently successful in elk country. And the sooner you realize the investment it takes, and the ingredients that need to go together to make your own success, the quicker you can be on your way to becoming a wise, old elk hunter yourself.

Planning a Hunt

Some hunters are beat before they ever set foot into their chosen patch of elk country. They might just as well have stayed home. This failure has nothing to do with how good or bad an elk hunter they happen to be. It has to do with

If you're looking to shoot a good bull, you've first got to find an area where there's a good bull to be found.

their ability to fulfill their expectations.

Whether you're a first-time elk hunter or a seasoned veteran, you have to talk to yourself—and be honest with yourself—and decide what you expect out of your elk hunting. If you want to meet your expectations, you've got to set those expectations first. And that begins long, long before you set foot into elk country.

The more I'm around out-of-state hunters, especially, the more I realize that planning a hunt is a problem. It requires some research. It requires some care. It requires some honest assessments of what you're looking for in the hunt itself and what you hope to take home at the end of it.

For nonresidents, that kind of planning may take a year or more before everything can be put together. You have to research the state where you plan to hunt. What are the licensing procedures? When are the deadlines for submitting license requests? If you are planning to hunt with an outfitter, which outfitter do you want? What area do you want to hunt? What are the physical realities of hunting in that area? Are you looking for a backcountry camp or more creature

Chapter Four

■ *ELK TACTICS*

comforts? And if you want to go hunting without an outfitter, what are the things you'll need to do that? Do you pack an elk out on your back? Are there people with horses you can hire? Are there places you can go where getting an elk out of the hunting area isn't such an ordeal? Is this once-in-a-lifetime hunt going to turn out to be your dream come true or a nightmare that will haunt you to the end of your hunting days?

Luckily, most fish and game departments in elk country have addresses and phone numbers that can give you a running start on these things. They have outfitter lists. They have people who can talk to you. They'll give you a starting point.

These are things that resident hunters, for the most part, don't have to deal with. If you're an every-year elk hunter, you generally have a routine. Even if you don't have a routine, you have better access to friends or acquaintances who can provide you with the information you need. But even resident hunters can't afford to overlook proper planning.

In my own case, if I'm planning to hunt in the September archery season of Montana, I'm already doing my planning in June. I'm out scouting the area I plan to hunt. I'm talking to other hunters who have hunted that place in September. I'm making my decisions about what I'm looking for in an elk that fall. Am I just going to put some good meat in the freezer? Am I going to hold out for a six-point? Am I going to hold out even longer and pass on the small and medium six-points and see if I can put an arrow into a real trophy-class bull?

All of these considerations will play a role in deciding when, where, and how you're going to hunt elk. But if you wait until you're actually in the field to make them, you're setting yourself up for a fall. It has always been my contention—and I've said it and written it before—that there is no such thing as a bad elk. Every elk out there in hunting season is an animal that would tickle some hunter to death, just to put his tag on it. There are guys I know who would rather hang a tag on a cow than any old bull, even a trophy. These guys are hunting for the high-quality meat that a cow invariably provides.

One guy told me about his college days back in the 1960s when he and some of his college buddies would specifically set goals of shooting a big calf. They didn't have much freezer space and couldn't handle a bigger elk without wasting the meat. And they found out that a calf elk provided meat that was so tender that not even the worst of college student cooks could screw it up when they cooked it. And, of course, there are the bull hunters. But is a spike good enough? How about a raghorn? How about a five-by-five? A six-by-six? A trophy six-by-six or seven-by-seven or eight-by-eight? You're the hunter now. You set the goals. Then, once you've set the goals, figure out how you're going to fulfill them. There's absolutely nothing in the hunting world that makes me sicker—or angrier—than a hunter who knocks an elk down and then isn't satisfied with what he sees when it's on the ground. Yet I've witnessed some horrible displays of hunting ethics over the years and even some temper tantrums. In truth, every elk deserves more respect than that. Any animal does. So set your goals first and then stick to them.

If you're looking for a classic case of how critical planning can be, look no further than a call I once got from a hunter in Colorado. To his credit, the hunter had set a goal for himself. To his credit also, the hunter had paid his dues and found success in the past, taking a five-by-six in the particular area he hunted. Now, the hunter had a new goal. He wanted very badly to shoot a trophy class bull.

His question was whether or not he could find a trophy bull in the area he had been hunting. It's not an easy question. The answers aren't so cut and dried. But you've got to look at the clues the hunter provided. He said he saw a lot of elk there. He saw a lot of small bulls and up to three hundred to five hundred head of cows a year. Was there a trophy bull there, too, that he just hadn't seen yet?

Without the benefit of knowing the area intimately—but after prodding the hunter with a few more questions—I found out that his hunting area followed a fairly common

Chapter Four

ELK TACTICS

Elk country can be an awfully big place, and it takes some knowledge of that big place to know where the elk are going to be.

profile of what you'll find in many elk states today. His area did have a lot of elk. But it also had a lot of hunters. A lot of elk were taken out of the area. But none of them were particularly large. The same scenario is heard in a lot of places. Normally, what we're seeing in many elk states—Colorado being one of them—is that a lot of elk are being produced, but that hunting pressure is taking the bulls out before they get a chance to reach trophy status. The hunter had worked this area for six years. The biggest bull he had shot was a six-by-five, which he had mounted. I told him he was probably battling some tall odds to take a bull that was bigger.

If you plan to take a bona fide trophy by most veteran hunters' standards, what you're looking for is one that scores 350 points on up. That requires a bull to have everything just right, and one of the key ingredients is enough age for his antlers to grow that big. For that, you'd need to find an area where bulls aren't shot as soon as they become legal. Hunting has to be limited by some factor. That factor might be limited-entry hunting—hunting by special permit only. The limiting factor might be restricted access. Or, perhaps, the limiting factor could be the country itself.

If you have to travel twenty to thirty miles on foot or horseback from the end of the road, that is generally a pretty good place to find a trophy elk. There may not be as many elk in there as there are in other areas. But there are definitely fewer hunters in there, too. As a result, the elk that do live there have a much better chance of reaching an age where they can grow big antlers. So my first piece of advice to the hunter would be to start doing the research and the field work to find another spot. Trophy bulls are rare jewels in the elk world. All the ingredients to make them have to be in place. And based on what he told me, the area he described lacked an important ingredient—age.

If the hunter was dead set on continuing to hunt the area he described, my advice was to find the most remote spot he could within that area. Find the spot with the best security. Find the place where the other hunters wouldn't go. Look for any little place that would give a bull a bit of an advantage over the hunters, where he might survive a few more years. While places like this are good places to look for bulls after the breeding season is done, they can play a key role in survival even when bulls' brains are fuzzied by their sex drive. Even in the breeding season, when bulls are drawn to the herds of cows and calves, they'll still try to pull into remote areas when they can. The draw of the breeding season isn't enough to make bulls totally foolish when they're faced with heavy hunting pressure. Even in areas with high hunter pressure, the bulls will get the breed-

Chapter Four

ELK TACTICS

ing done. But they're more likely to do it at night, moving in with the cows and calves after dark and moving out before daylight. Then, after a night of breeding and being harassed by younger bulls, they'll pull back into tough little pockets of cover during daylight hours when hunters are about. If the hunter was set on staying in his home country, those remote areas are the places I'd look for a trophy. And I'd be ready to look long and hard and maybe still not find one.

This need to get everything right, and to have all the ingredients in place, can even vary by the year. To grow big antlers, you need good genetics, good nutrition, and longevity. If you mess around with any of the three factors, you don't get a trophy bull. And one factor alone can make a huge difference.

A friend of mine was lucky enough to get an elk tag to hunt in Arizona a few years back. I was lucky enough that he asked me to go along with him and try to shoot some film of the hunt.

Arizona has a reputation for producing some giant bulls. My friend knew this. He also knew that, for him, it was going to be the hunt of a lifetime in that state. As a seasoned elk hunter, he planned to make the most of it. He set his goals very high. And, to his credit, he lived up to those goals. The problem was that he never saw an elk that met them.

That wasn't his fault. It wasn't really Arizona's fault, either. It was just a combination of factors that foiled his plans. For Arizona, it had been an unusual year. It turned out all the bulls of any size all had real heavy first, second and third points and sometimes fourth points, but the fifth and sixth points were weak. With the fifth and sixth points being weak, the length of the antler was weak, as well. It was a situation he saw time after time, with each new elk that we called in.

After analyzing it, I realized that everyone in that area was complaining about the lack of rainfall that year and the low-water situation. It was almost like a drought. What did that do to the elk? The way I figured it, when the elk grew the first part of their antlers—the eyeguards, then the second point, then the third point, things had been all right. In the early part of the year, there had been enough moisture. The elk had tremendous growth, as usual, because of the good grass and ample water that the moisture had provided. But when it was time for the fourth point, main beam, fifth point, and sixth point to grow on their antlers, moisture conditions had turned sour. It had turned into a drought, of sorts, and the feed and water weren't so good. As a result, the top portion of the antlers hadn't grown so well. That top portion just looked like it had died.

As a result, the antlers weren't the giants that my friend was looking for. He couldn't find a big elk, no matter how hard he looked. He could find respectable elk, but not the trophy-class elk. And he went home without one.

In retrospect, you could call it a fluke. Many of those bulls we saw would have had trophy-class antlers the year before. The next year, if there was a wet season and good grass all year long, they'd have a good set of antlers again, with solid growth all the way to the top. But that year, feed conditions overrode even the good heredity that the Arizona bulls are famous for. It was just the wrong year to plan a hunt to Arizona.

If you're planning to hunt trophy bull elk, you had also better be able to judge what's a trophy and what's not. That judgment can come by looking at a lot of elk antlers in the field while they're still on a bull's head. It can come by looking at a lot of photos of trophy bulls. It can come by looking at trophy displays at sports shows or Rocky Mountain Elk Foundation banquets, or at enough sporting goods stores, motels, restaurants, or bars in elk country.

One of the better spot lessons I ever had in judging elk antlers came from a pair of shed antlers that my nephew and I found near Gardiner. It was in the spring of the year, the time when bulls shed their antlers and prepare to grow a new set. I got up early that day and climbed a mountain while it was still shrouded in fog.

I was trying to film some of the bulls that were just starting to lose their antlers. But when I got there, I found out that, with the fog, I couldn't see fifty yards in front of me.

Chapter Four

ELK TACTICS

There was a group of elk on the other side of a canyon from me, so I got my cow call out. At the sound, they picked their heads up. Then I heard some running sounds coming out of the fog. And here she came, a cow elk running right for me. Right behind her was a bunch of bulls, one of them a nice seven-point, a decent bull that would have qualified as a trophy to almost any elk hunter. The cow and bulls ran up to me, then ran past, apparently unaware of exactly where the sound was coming from.

As I continued on, the fog started to lift and another bunch of elk came down the hill. In the group was a big, mature, six-point with just one antler. As I was filming him, he shook his head and the antler shot off, straight up into the air. When it broke, it sounded like someone snapping a stick. When it came down, it landed right beside him and spooked him. The bull looked at the antler and shook his head, like he was trying to clear out the cobwebs. It was something I'd seen before. When bulls lose their antlers, it's like they get dizzy. When the bull left, he just started wandering off in a different direction while the other elk crossed the draw. The bull was wading through snow up to his chest, acting like he was goofy. It seemed to take him a while to get over the lightheadedness and return to the main group.

Later, I was telling the tale to my nephew, describing where it happened, how it happened, and exactly what the bull looked like. My nephew told me he had seen that one-antlered bull earlier, near where he was working, and had set out to find the first antler that was shed. And he found it. My nephew gave the antler to me, and I took it home. It was a perfect match for the one I had in terms of its points and conformation. But the antler I picked up weighed 13 pounds. The antler he picked up weighed 11 pounds. The difference was that one of the elk's antlers was smaller than the other. If you had been hunting for a trophy by record-book standards, you would have faced a huge deduction in Boone and Crockett or Pope and Young points.

The lesson was a bit of an eye-opener, even for someone accustomed to looking at lots of elk and able to judge tro-

Environmental conditions, as well as genetics, play a big role in determining how antlers will develop on a bull.

Chapter Four

phies pretty well. At a distance, just by looking at the antlers, you'd never have known there would be so much difference in weight. You never would have picked up on the discrepancy until you had the elk on the ground and got a close look.

For a hunter whose goal was to take a big six-point, that elk would have been enough. For someone who wanted to make the book, it would have been a huge disappointment.

In judging trophies, however, you've got to be exact. And you've got to know what you're looking for. You want the antler to be a massive, heavy-looking antler to start with. You have to know that the longest point of all is the fourth point—then look to make sure there are at least two points beyond that. Then you want to look at those fifth and sixth points to make sure you have good mass and length. Those fifth and sixth points will have to be eleven, twelve, or even thirteen inches long to score well. Make sure there's some size to the third point, too, because that's the one that is often weak. If you're looking for a trophy bull, you also have to consider the main beam. A good, long, mature main beam will go back toward a bull's flank. Sometimes, you'll see antlers that go clear to the hind quarters. When you're seeing that, you're looking at fifty-five- and sixty-inch main beams. To have a trophy and get into the record book, they have to be fifty-five-inch main beams.

Finally, make sure that all the points are there and that none are broken off. All too often, a hunter will think he has a trophy only to find out that an eyeguard is broken off, but in the excitement of looking at the mass and size of all the other points, the hunter just didn't notice.

One of the hardest things for a hunter to do is to judge a trophy-class bull when there is only a short time in which to make that judgment. It's a flash judgment, one you have to make quickly, when you jump a bull or see a bull for an instant and know you have to shoot or it will be gone. If you're just looking for a nice, respectable trophy, it's not so critical to judge point after point. You want to make sure he has all the points and none of them are broken. Usually you can do that pretty quickly. But I've seen guys who will shoot too fast and end up with a trophy bull that's missing a point or two. Often, that creates the most pathetic of all scenes. I've seen some guys actually kick the elk and be mad. If they had been that concerned about the trophy, they should have looked at it a little closer before they shot it. After a guy shoots an elk, it's his elk and it's his trophy and he should respect that. It's really discouraging to see a guy shoot one and have him start complaining that it's not big enough. And you don't gain much respect from other hunters by doing it, either.

Hunters who aren't quite so picky have it a lot easier—especially in an area that has a number of bulls. If you have an area where you have a lot of bulls together, with a quick glance, you can tell which ones are the bigger ones. They just seem to stand out above and beyond all the rest. That's especially true if you know a little about the genetics of the elk in the area you're hunting. In particular areas, bulls often seem to follow a genetic profile. Maybe your area has a lot of tall-antlered bulls. Maybe it has a lot of wide-antlered bulls. Maybe the big bulls of that area are known for the mass of their antlers, even if they're not so long and tall.

When we were hunting bulls in Wyoming a couple of years ago, the thing that was misleading in judging the elk there was that, genetically, they were all so high at the shoulders. They were extremely tall-bodied elk. I measured one that was five feet, ten inches at the shoulders and another that was six-foot-two. The tallness of the animals tended to make their antlers look smaller in proportion. The genetics of that area also dictated that the bulls' racks weren't very wide. They were tall, too.

We found that a couple of these elk dressed out at 850 and 890 pounds, field-dressed. That put their live weight at over 1,000 pounds. They were just big-bodied elk. As a result, their antlers didn't look that big when you were glassing them at a distance. Their antlers didn't look out of proportion to their bodies. But when you got the elk on the ground and got up close to them, you realized how big their antlers were. In some parts of elk country, just the reverse can be

Chapter Four

true. If you have small-bodied elk, even medium-sized antlers can look huge. It's all a matter of knowing the elk of your area.

I can't stress enough how important it is that the hunter know what kind of elk he wants to shoot. And if the expectations change as the hunt progresses, that's fine, too, just as long as a hunter is honest with himself about it.

I've known a lot of hunters who start out with the highest of expectations and the greatest of goals as to what they're going to shoot—it's the biggest trophy bull of all time or nothing. But as the hunt goes on, the goals change and the bull gets smaller and smaller and smaller. That's understandable. But realize that the first bull you see may turn out to be the biggest you see, too. And if your goals are too high and you decide not to shoot, you may be kicking yourself later.

If you don't take the first elk, that's fine. If you decide to kick yourself later, that's fine, too. Heck, you can even kick your hunting partner, if he'll put up with it. Just remember, it's up to you to set your goals. You have the expectations. You have to attain them. But whatever you do, be happy and please don't kick the elk after you've pulled the trigger.

The Setup

So you've got your patch of real estate selected, eh? It holds the elk of your dreams. You know that because you've done your homework, planned your hunt carefully, and done your scouting of elk within that area. But now that you've got the real estate, what do you do with it?

Already, I've alluded to many of the things you should and shouldn't do in elk country. You and I have chatted a bit about some of the pitfalls. We've talked about why elk will be in certain areas at certain times of the day. We've dissected your chosen mountain and know the bedding areas, the feeding areas, and all the trails in between.

If you're hunting in rifle season and simply want to ambush an elk, the setup involves finding a spot where the elk are likely to be at a certain time of day. That may be as

A hunter has to have a clear path in front of him, both to see the elk that are there and to get a shot at them.

simple as getting a bunch of your hunting partners to push through a patch of timber and for you and a buddy to cover an escape route. If you don't have enough hunters in your group, try to get a read on other hunters in the area and let them push the elk toward you. Or the setup may be to pattern the elk for a few days, locate the areas where they feed out into at dusk or pass through early in the morning, and wait there for them to do it again.

For people interested in calling elk, the setup becomes a bit more complicated. It also becomes far more critical to hunting success.

Probably one of the biggest downfalls of people doing good calling, as opposed to bad calling, is not the sounds

Chapter Four

■ ELK TACTICS

they're making, but the bad setup they choose to make their first calls. When I say a bad setup, it means you're in a place that an animal would probably not be. You want to be in a place where an animal would normally be. You also want to be in an area where the animals are comfortable being called. For example, if you were in a timbered area that bordered an open flat, you'd need to work somewhere near the edge of that timber. If you went to the far end of the flat and expected the animals to come out of the timber and cross the open flat, you'd be in the wrong place.

For the most part, elk are more comfortable in timber. Timber provides them with security cover during the day. They'll move around in the timber, and even in small openings in the timber, far more easily than they will out in the open.

Of course, you can get carried away with that idea, too. If you hope to get a shot at an animal, you don't want to be in timber that's too dense. Believe it or not, that works against you in two ways. When an elk comes in, you can't see him—that's the first strike. But a second problem is that when the elk comes in, he can't see the elk that's making the noise, either—that's strike two. Even on the off-chance you do get a shot, it probably isn't going to be a clear shot—that's strike three. So get out.

In situations where the timber is too dense, chances are you'll get into a situation where, as they say, the elk has hung up on you. The elk comes in just so far. Then you can't seem to bring him in that extra distance that you need to get a good shot, or a clear shot. It's a classic tragedy for a hunter. The elk doesn't see you. He doesn't spook. But he doesn't come close enough. And if you do move much trying to get a better position, the elk will likely see you because he is so close. The answer is to not set up in areas with dense timber.

So where should you set up to call? To start with, you've got to locate an area where the elk are likely to be. That's a given. If there aren't any elk within earshot, you're not going to call one in. Beyond that constraint, I'll tell you that I have had excellent luck calling at the edge of little open parks or in what I like to call more scattered timber, where visibility was somewhat limited, but both the animals and I could still see fairly well.

A second rule of thumb is to call from a position above the elk. Setting up above the elk will give you a number of advantages. For one thing, elk are far more comfortable coming up a slope to a caller. For some reason, they don't mind coming up. Calling from the same elevation as the elk is the next-best option. Trying to call an elk down to you is by far the worst choice. Aside from the elk's tendencies to want to come up, calling from above, especially in fairly open timber, gives you the advantage of good visibility. You can see farther. You can spot elk at a longer distance. If you can see the elk and how they respond to your calling, you can adjust your calling to better bring them in.

The third rule of thumb is to make sure you're in a position not just to shoot, but to get a clear, uncluttered shot. Too often, this is another part of the setup where a hunter fails. For some reason, hunters feel they have to surround themselves with cover. They almost have to create a duck-blind type of situation. They have to find a tight little hole in the cover and crawl in. The trouble with this is that a tight little blind can be hard to shoot from, especially if you have to raise a bow and draw it back. As a result, I don't like to be locked into underbrush that I can't move around in or shoot out of.

My answer has always been to set up in front of the cover, using the cover behind me to break up my outline. Then I try to get low. For whatever the reason, the sight of a man standing upright has always acted like a danger sign to elk. Things low to the ground don't seem to bother them so much. So I keep a low profile. Most of the time, I'm calling from a kneeling position. Lying flat on the ground is even better. If I'm kneeling, that's a position from which I can shoot a bow or a rifle. I know I can—I practice shooting from the kneeling position. If you're lying on the ground, you simply have to be more patient. You can wait until the animal turns, or his head is behind a tree, then get into a position to shoot.

Chapter Four

■ ELK TACTICS

Just because you feel you're more in the open when you're out in front of a patch of cover, rather than being buried inside, doesn't mean you'll spook the elk. For whatever the reason, as long as you're still, it doesn't seem to bother them. And just as long as you keep a low profile, you'll look more like a lump on the ground or the stump of a tree than you'll look like a living, breathing hunter.

While we're on the topic of exactly where to set up, and how elk are so keenly aware of movement, let's explore that just a bit further. A lot of people feel that, once you make your setup and once you begin your elk calling, you shouldn't move at all. For me, at least, that has never been the case. Some may call me a victim of nervous energy—I can't seem to stay pinned to one exact spot for a long time—but that isn't the reason I move around. A lot of times, I'll start calling and, after I've called a bit, I'll begin looking the country over and find a spot that's a little bit better nearby. I'll move there. As long as you don't have an elk close, you can get away with some movement. But I'll move at a slow pace, not get up and run. Sometimes, I'll even move on my hands and knees and ease into the new position.

That small amount of movement—especially if you know more than one elk sound to make on your call—can give the appearance of more elk being in the area. If you're working with a lovesick bull, that little bit of added appeal may just be enough to bring him in. Even if it doesn't, you've worked your way into a better position to see elk and, perhaps, to get a shot at the elk you see.

One aspect of a setup that's often overlooked is the scent a hunter leaves behind. These animals have an incredible sense of smell. Elk, deer, and other animals can smell where you've walked. For that reason, think about the route that the elk may take as they respond to your calling. Try to make sure that elk aren't following the same path. If the elk are wary, your smell may stop them in their tracks.

A prime example of animals' sense of smell was shown to me on a coyote hunt where we didn't concentrate enough on our setup. We knew about where the coyotes were. But

If you want elk to respond to your calling, you have to make sure you move into your setup location undetected.

we didn't enter the calling site from the right angle. We called anyway. It didn't take long before a pair of coyotes came in at a dead run. The lead coyote, which we figured was the male, ran in to about two hundred yards and immediately started to work toward the downwind side of us. When he hit our scent, at a dead run, he did a complete 180,

Chapter Four

swapped end for end, and ran straight back away from us without even hesitating.

With elk, the same thing applies. If they pick up your scent, whether it's on the ground or in the air, it automatically puts them on the alert. Depending on hunting pressure and the mood of the elk at the time, they may tolerate it a bit, or they may do exactly what that coyote did. I've seen elk, in areas where they weren't pressured at all, that tolerated the smell of a man fairly well. If a bull was hot at the peak of the rut, he'd come in anyway. But I've seen it just the other way, too, where a perfect setup was foiled by a wayward gust of wind or a wary elk crossing the trail I came in on. The best solution is to try to arrange your setup so the wind and your tracks don't give you away.

Why worry so much about the setup? Why try to make everything perfect? For one thing, if you set up correctly, you'll stand a better chance of calling in an elk. But beyond that, think about what happens when you don't set up correctly. An elk hears your calling and responds to it. He comes in close. He finds a man instead of another elk. That elk is going to be far more difficult to fool the next time around. If he comes in at all, he's going to come in as a far more wary elk. Educate him enough with too many bad setups and bad situations, and he may just refuse to come in, no matter how good you sound or how good your setup may be.

That's one of the reasons why I pay so much attention to the setup in the first place. And, perhaps, it's why I get so frustrated with hunters who don't pay any attention to the setup at all. If a hunter is just wandering through the mountains, calling anywhere and everywhere, and just making elk sounds to hear the elk call back to him, he's doing little more than making it tougher for me—and you.

Now, before you get too gun shy about calling and worry too much about your setup, don't think that you have to have a bull elk standing right in front of you before you start calling. It's enough just to have some suspicions. Perhaps it's fresh sign. Perhaps it's an area that you know holds elk. Perhaps it's just the time of day when you suspect elk will be in a favored bedding area and should be responsive to calling.

Sometimes, hunters wait too long and wait until they're too close to the elk before they start calling. If you get too close and then blow a call—especially a bull sound—you may blow the animals right out of there. Bulls, especially bulls in the rut, don't seem to like that kind of a surprise. If a bull is coming in on them, they'd just as soon know about it a little ahead of time. One tactic that I've used successfully over the years in situations like that is to make a high-pitched bugle from quite a distance away. It's not a challenge call. It's just something of a high-pitched squeal to let the bull know that there's another bull in the area. I try to establish myself as another bull that's moving in toward them. Of course, when I make these calls, I try to make sure it's from a good setup. You never know when that bull might come out to meet the challenger.

Another good time to look for a good place for a setup is when you see other elk. If you can find some cows or calves anytime just before, during, or after the rut, odds are that there's a bull with them somewhere in the area. The bull may be quite close. He may be one hundred or two hundred or more yards away, but he's keeping track of them. If he is a little distance away, he may even be more responsive to the high-pitched squeals and cow sounds when he figures another bull is moving in on his cows or, perhaps, that a cow of his has tried to wander away. Bulls like that can come in a hurry. You had better be ready with the right setup.

We've talked about not hiding yourself behind trees and giving yourself a good field of view and good range of shooting motion. We've also talked about how fast those elk can come in. Last fall, in Wyoming, the reasons for this were hammered home once again. There were three of us in the hunting group. One was a bowhunter. Another was the caller. I was doing the filming.

When we set up, the bowhunter chose to hide behind a tree, about twenty-five yards in front of us, while we did the calling and filming. In this instance, a six-point bull

Chapter Four

ELK TACTICS

Some animals, like this coyote, are born to be stealthy, and hunters have much to learn from them.

responded quickly and came in fast. But when the bull came in, he was on the opposite side of the tree, in a little opening about ten yards away. In order to get a shot, the bowhunter had to step out from behind the tree. That spooked the bull, and he jumped about five yards to his left, again placing himself behind the tree. In what can only be described as a sad case of cat and mouse, the hunter went back to his original position. So did the elk, who was once again behind the tree. But because of the movement, the bull was really edgy now. So was the hunter—he had a heavy-duty adrenaline rush. In the end, the hunter never did get a shot. The bull went wide around the hunter and came in to the caller and me—and we weren't shooting, either. So the lesson of the story is not to play cat and mouse behind trees. Get out there where you can shoot and keep a low profile when you do it.

So far, the only reasons we've discussed for making the right setup to call elk have been for effective elk hunting and to avoid educating the elk and ruining it for other hunters. But there is at least one other reason for making sure you've got good visibility when you set up to call and aren't buried somewhere in a dense tangle of timber. Let's see if you can figure it out while I tell you a little story.

The tale takes place in June. I was out looking for some bulls to do some filming. About June, the elk bulls and cows split up. The cows spread out and drop calves, then get into big cow-calf herds. The bulls head off on their own, following the lush green grass to higher country where the winds blow a bit harder and it isn't quite so warm and the flies aren't nearly so pesky.

For whatever the reason, the bulls weren't cooperating with me. They became more skittish. I didn't get the good film footage I was looking for. I was beginning to get a little frustrated at a whole lot of effort on my part with very few results to show for it. I was going up through one of the open meadows, trying to work them, when I saw a bear at the other end of the meadow. It was a black bear. With the opportunity to perhaps get a little film footage for my efforts, I pulled out a cow call that I had along. I knew for myself, and had heard from many others, that predators do respond to cow calls. Now, I'd get a chance to verify it on film.

When I blew my call, the bear raised his head, but went about his business. He was snipping the tops of the flowers off. I blew the call again, and again I got his attention. But still, he kept minding his own business. He never looked like he was coming in to me. For my part, I didn't want to

ELK TACTICS

get aggressive. If you do distress calls of a calf—or of a fawn, if you're using a deer call—predators come in right away. The bear just slowly worked his way in my general direction. He looked like he was minding his own business.

But when the bear got to within about fifty yards from me, he knew where the sound was coming from. I was down on my knees. At that point, he lowered his head and started swinging it from side to side and started walking right toward me. I thought he saw me—he's not going to come all the way in. But he kept coming. Finally, I raised up and said, "Hey, bear." At this point, he was only twenty yards away. By that time, my adrenaline was pumping pretty well. For the bear's part, he didn't leave. He stood up and looked at me. Then he dropped back down and the hair down his neck and back was standing straight up—similar to the hair on the back of my neck and my head.

Finally, he turned around and left at a run, after he got a view of what I was. I was hoping and praying he would keep on running. A lot of times when you have a bear that leaves you, he'll run about twenty yards and stop. Then he looks over the situation. That is when you have to be prepared. If he comes the second time, he's going to come all the way. I had my fingers crossed, my toes crossed, my legs crossed. And he didn't come. He turned and went the other way.

But it was a near-enough situation that I got to thinking about all the times you're in bear country and you're using calls. If you're in dense timber where you don't have a good field of view, how close is that bear going to be before you see him? And how are you going to react when that bear stands up closer than twenty yards away from you? If you're making sounds like an elk, the bear is coming in looking for a meal. And if the situation turns sour, that bear could just as soon be making a meal of you. Having a good setup with a good field of view is one way to avoid that happening. You won't just be able to keep better track of the elk as they come in. You will be able to keep better track of anything that's responding to your calls.

It wasn't the only time I'd ever run into a bear, of course. And in my part of elk country, bears you run into aren't always blacks. One time, I was bugling in a basin, far into the backcountry where we'd ridden on horseback. The elk we were calling were on the far side of the basin, and that's where we'd been concentrating our attentions. Suddenly, we heard some rustling in the brush behind us and turned around, and there was a grizzly standing up on his hind legs. Right then and there, when the horses spotted him, we just about had a rodeo. On the other hand, when the bear spotted the horses, he realized they weren't elk. He had apparently seen enough hunters and horses before. As a result, he took off. But that grizzly was plenty close enough, too, about forty yards from us. And believe me, when you're sitting there with just bows and arrows and a grizzly is standing up that close eyeing you, it's a helpless feeling. I pack a good brand of pepper spray along, and I wouldn't hesitate to use it. But, given the choice, I'd rather have known there was a grizzly eyeballing us from more than forty yards away and not have had to worry about using the pepper spray. Guys say it works. I hope I never have to find out.

One final word of advice about creating the proper setup for calling is to not become discouraged. In the end, calling is a pretty fickle undertaking. Sometimes, you'll go out and do some calling and might call all day and not get a single animal in. You might do fifteen or twenty setups in a day and never budge an elk. There are days like that.

Other times, you can bring in an elk when all signs would indicate that an elk should never set foot within a mile of you. The wind is swirling your scent all around. Your visibility isn't just right. You begin calling and the elk are above you, you're calling from down below, and there's nothing you can do about it. And still, the elk come in.

Nobody can explain it. For some of the elk that don't respond, we blame it on animals that are being overcalled and are not responsive. There are too many guys calling. But you might go there another day, do the same things, and the elk come in. That, we explain away by the fact that the bulls were really hot that day.

Chapter Four

ELK TACTICS

The bottom line is that even ideal situations don't always work. And some situations that are less than ideal work out just fine. For me, I just figure there are simply a lot of variables in elk hunting—and in elk calling in particular—that we still don't fully understand. We're learning. We still have a lot to learn. But one of the things I've learned over the years is that making the right setup will greatly increase your odds of calling in an elk in the first place, and getting a shot at the elk once it arrives. And along the way, it'll help you avoid those close encounters with bears, too.

Elk that are pressured will still do all the things elk do, like battling other bulls, but will be extremely wary of hunters.

Dealing with Problem Elk

The bull was somewhere in the broad timbered basin below me. And he was hot! Each time I'd bugle, my sounds wouldn't even have finished before he was quickly answering back. The wind was in my face. There was a drizzly rain falling to dull my scent in case the wind swirled. There wasn't another hunter for miles. Everything was just perfect. But the bull didn't seem interested in coming any closer.

As I slowly worked my way closer to him, calling intermittently, the bull continued to answer. But then things changed. The bull must have figured that flight was better than fight. He was moving off, several hundred yards out in front of me. As I hustled to catch up, he must have been hustling a bit, too, to keep that distance between us. With a bow and arrows, I'd have to cut the distance down a lot. I'd have to get a whole lot closer. So I started moving more quickly, bugling less often. All I wanted was to catch up to him or, better yet, to get out in front of him. I bugled just often enough to keep track of him. But I never caught up. I just couldn't move fast enough to outpace an elk.

It's a scenario that unfolds often in elk country. Bulls choose flight over fight. They'd just as soon gather up their cows and save what they've got, rather than face another bull that just might try to take those cows away.

That's one example of a problem elk. There are many others. Based on the letters I've gotten and the hunters I've talked to, problem elk of one kind or another are everywhere these days. And as hunting pressure continues to rise, expect problem elk to become even more common in the future.

In that little story above, my biggest problem was that I was working an area that had been heavily hunted before I got there, even though no other hunters were there that day. The bull, as hot as he was, had been called to by hunters on other occasions and had learned from those experiences. Even though my setup was fine, something had gone wrong. Maybe I relied too much on my bull call. Maybe he figured it was a lose-lose situation, whether the call was from another bull or a hunter. One might take his cows, the other might take him. Maybe the bull was just testing that new bull he heard to see if he'd react the way other hot bulls react, if he'd keep following the herd. If I had only followed long enough and far enough and gotten close enough, perhaps the bull would have turned and come in to answer the challenge.

As it turned out, none of those things ever had a chance to play themselves out. After moving about a half-mile in pursuit of the bull—and with the bull still moving out in front of me—another bull snuck in from the side. I caught just enough motion out of the corner of my eye to stop my pursuit and turn. What I saw was a satellite bull coming in si-

Chapter Four

lently. As it turned out, it was a pretty nice satellite bull, too—a decent six-point. If he was smaller than the herd bull I was calling, then I can only imagine how big that herd bull must have been. As it was, I settled for the satellite, which never made a sound, but kept coming to within twenty-five yards before I put an arrow into him and ended the hunt.

Among the lessons I learned from the experience was that doing the right thing, and continuing to do the right thing, will reap dividends. Persistence pays off. Patience in almost any form pays off, too. It may not always produce the results you expect, but the results can still be very satisfactory.

One of the hallmarks of today's problem elk is that they have become increasingly silent. They have associated calling with humans. They have found out that if they remain silent, a lot of those humans will give themselves away, or simply go away. The hunters will ruin the situation for themselves. They'll identify themselves as humans. And the elk will sneak away unscathed.

I'm reminded of a radio-collared elk that a biologist told me about years ago. The biologist had the benefit of a receiver that he used to track the bull. Without it, he admitted, he probably never would have known where the elk was. How could he be so sure? Well, there were dozens of hunters who never spotted the bull, even though they passed within fifty yards of him.

The bull had holed up in a little patch of dense timber, not more than twenty yards wide in any direction, about fifty yards off a county road. Some hunters drove that road. Others were on foot, hiking to other places. All were more interested in traveling than they were in hunting. None of them bothered to push that little patch of dense timber. And the bull elk laid up there all day long, watching the parade go by.

Have elk always done this to hunters? In some respects, yes, they have. A number of big satellite bulls have always had a tendency to go silent—even before the current onslaught of hunters. Those elk must have learned their lessons of silence by being kicked around once or twice too often by herd bulls when they sang out a challenge. By going silent, they prevented the herd bull from knowing where they were lurking. As a result, they could sometimes sneak off with a cow at the edge of the herd.

But the universality of silent elk is something new. There are more silent bulls now than ever before. They've learned that the old strategy of not being picked on by the herd bull works equally well to avoid having arrows or bullets sent in their direction.

Elk like this can be called in. Well, perhaps not all of them can be called in. But certainly a lot of them can. But if you want to call them, then you, as a hunter, have to be as close to perfect in your approach as it's possible for you to be.

Why so perfect? Simply because so many other hunters ahead of you have been so imperfect. They've given the elk a living library of all the mistakes it's possible for a hunter to make. And call the elk smart or call them dumb animals, but the elk remember. They've watched hunters stand on ridgetops and make elk calls. They've smelled the place where a hunter was calling from. They've winded hunters. Perhaps they've even had an arrow or a bullet sent in their direction just to emphasize the point.

The bottom line is that you've got to pay attention to every aspect of your hunt. You've got to approach the entire elk hunting situation with the same attitude as if you were stalking a wary elk. That begins with literally sneaking through elk country, quietly moving to positions where you can glass the areas ahead of you, slipping into calling positions without the elk seeing you. Then, when you're ready to call, you have to pay close attention to the sounds you're making. You have to play the silent game yourself, to some extent, and hold your calling to only the sounds that will be effective for you.

It wasn't like this in the old days when elk weren't so wary. With less-than-wary elk, you could get away with blasting out a big, loud, cow sound or a full bugle with grunts. With less-than-wary elk, they'd just answer you. Sometimes, they might even come in. But if you try the same approach with wary elk, you can turn even a good

Chapter Four

situation sour very quickly.

Instead, I like to take a more quiet approach. I'll usually start out with a cow sound, not too loud. Cow sounds aren't quite so intimidating. Quiet cow sounds won't shock the elk out of the country, either, if they happen to be nearby. If no elk responds, I might increase the volume of the cow sounds a bit, but the key is still to call sparingly. With wary elk, especially, you don't want to overdo it. When I do mix in a bull sound, it will be just a short, high-pitched squeal. That's a bull sound, but not an intimidating bull sound. If an elk doesn't respond, but I still figure there are elk in the area, I'll go back to the cow sounds from then on.

Calling wary elk in situations like this becomes something of an exercise in faith—you have to have faith in your calling ability and your knowledge of elk in the area you're calling. Often, the elk will not make a sound, even if there are bulls and cows in the area. You've got to exercise your patience in situations like this. You've got to stick with it a long, long time. And most of that time you will simply be sitting there, or kneeling there, looking for elk that aren't talking back to you.

I've also learned that I've got to limit the number of setups that I make when I'm hunting problem elk. The Missouri Breaks of Montana are a prime example. The Breaks are hunted very heavily during bow season, which coincides with the rut there. And every bowhunter in the Breaks seems to have a pocketful of elk calls. As a result, the elk's reactions to the calls isn't anything like those of unwary elk. In fact, I've often figured that when a hunter calls, rather than responding, the elk talk among themselves agreeing on which manufacturer and what model call the hunter is using.

Art Hobart, a hunting partner, found that calls will work there, but you've got to use them extremely sparingly. One soft cow sound, maybe two. Then perhaps not another single sound for a half hour. If there are elk within earshot that you can't see, they'll hear the call. But they'll come in to it ever-so-slowly. Most often, they'll come in without answering back. They'll come in, even to soft cow sounds, ex-

Hunters are going to have to be much more precise in what they do if they hope to lure in a good bull.

tremely warily. And there's a real premium in the Breaks on knowing where the elk are likely to go and putting yourself in their path. Problem elk are most difficult to move in directions that they don't want to go.

Hobart and others in the Breaks have worked elk more

Chapter Four

ELK TACTICS

aggressively than that, but the more aggressive calling is always reserved for elk you can see. With those elk, you can watch their reactions and know when to call and when to lay off.

In situations like this, I've found that your best strategy is to make absolutely sure that you've got a good setup before you begin calling. That may mean you only make one or two good setups a day. If the weather conditions are bad—high winds or elk holing up in rain or snow storms—I may not call at all.

Believe me, that's a far better strategy than making a dozen poor setups a day. Or, even worse, walking through the forest and calling every one hundred to two hundred yards. Ineffective calling only educates elk about calls. It makes it tougher for you and for all those who follow you. That's how problem elk are created. So my best advice is to concentrate on the setup, make sure it's perfect, and then call sparingly. And exercise patience to the utmost. Stick with that setup long beyond the point when you figure an elk would respond.

As I've mentioned before, I'm not the most patient person in situations like this. It's tough for me to simply sit and wait for elk I don't see. So I've learned to rely on my watch and I'll make a point to check it when I start calling. After I've sat there for a long, long time, I'll look at the watch again and find that only ten minutes have passed. As I said, patience doesn't come easy for me. I'd rather be walking and stalking. That's why I always go by my watch to make sure I've given a good area a chance. Patience. Sparse calling. Those are key words to remember. Sometimes, all it takes is a call or two, but those calls need to be spaced out and you have to wait long enough for the silent elk to find you.

Another thing I'll pay attention to is the quality of the sounds I'm making. That's something the old-timers never really had to worry about. In the old days, when calls were much more crude than the models on the market today, it was pretty easy to pick out the real elk sounds from the sounds of humans trying to make elk sounds. An elk whistle sounded like an elk whistle. A grunt tube often delivered far more human grunting than it did elk grunts. Some guys were really, really good. But a lot of them were awful, too. And at the time, the elk weren't so call-wise, either. Today, some of the better sounds you'll hear are coming from the callers. In truth, some real elk sound much worse. But callers have to be better with their sounds. Bull sounds have to be precise. Cow sounds need to be accurate, too. They have to be especially accurate for problem elk.

One of the ways to help insure that your sounds are good is to stick with simple sounds. After listening to thousands of elk bugle over the years, I realize that elk can make a wide range of noises. Today's elk calls, both the diaphragm types and the reed type, can make just about all of them. But just because real elk are making all those sounds doesn't mean that you have to make them. Keeping your calling short, sweet, and simple will lessen the chances of you hitting a sour note that will spook a problem elk. And those simple sounds will work just fine in fooling an elk into coming in.

The old standby of elk callers—pressing elk into action by following them relentlessly—still works, too. But you've got to be a bit more careful about this tactic with problem elk. Elk that move out on you can still be followed, pressing them and pushing them, in hopes that they'll finally turn around and come to your calls. But look for the elk to go farther and faster in their flight. Look to them to be more reluctant to turn and come in. And plan to use more mild coaxing than aggressive challenging if you hope to make that bull turn.

By far, the best chance you'll have to bring that bull elk in is if you can somehow get ahead of him. Calling an elk in a direction it wants to go is infinitely easier than turning him back in a direction where he doesn't. One hunter I know literally runs through the mountains to get ahead of elk that are moving out. His tactic has worked for him, too. But this guy is in incredible shape. He doesn't mind running up and down those slopes. And there have been many times when even he couldn't run down an elk.

Chapter Four

ELK TACTICS

Another tactic that works effectively with problem elk, if you're hunting with a partner, is to split up. Wary elk will often only come in just so far. They'll hang up somewhere out in front of you. They'll stop there and not come in that final twenty-five or fifty or one hundred yards that would allow you to take a shot. The answer is to put the shooter in a forward position, twenty-five or fifty or one hundred yards in front of the caller. The task of the shooter is to keep his eyes open and make sure he's in a position to see the elk coming in. That shooter has to be stealthy. He has to be quiet. He has to employ all the fine hunting skills. But if he is stealthy and quiet and skillful, he can adjust his position to elk that are answering the caller behind him.

Sometimes, when an elk does come in, but only comes in so far, it's a good tactic for the caller to pull back, leaving the shooter out in front. As the caller pulls back, he entices the bull to come in closer. As the bull comes in, he bumps into the shooter.

This shooter and caller system should increase your odds of getting a chance at a problem elk. But then elk are famous for going against all odds, too. The caller has to be stealthy and quiet and skillful, too, because all too often, a silent bull sneaks in on him, somehow getting around the shooter. If the caller isn't ready to take the shot, an opportunity can slip away awfully easily.

Another thing to remember is that elk, during the rut, are typically moving in groups. If you locate one elk, there are very likely others nearby. Perhaps just one elk is answering you, but others are in the area. One of the others may slip in silently to investigate.

One of the worst things you can do is to call and then leave an area too soon. If you leave and the elk come in after you've left, you've probably spoiled that elk for future calling. Elk that do come in late will simply smell the scent you've left behind and learn to associate calling with humans. You've simply educated the elk to be wary of calls.

If you're archery hunting, the same thing could be said of blowing elk calls periodically as you move along. That will

There's nothing more important than patience, sticking with a good setup and a good location, and waiting for an elk to come in.

only create more problem elk. If an elk sees you, all you're doing is alerting the animal that you're in the area. For rifle hunters, that may not be exactly true. With the added range of a rifle, you may force an elk to stand up in its bed, at which point you'll see it and get a shot at one hundred yards. But with the limited range of a bow, the same thing can't be said.

The bottom line for calling to problem elk is to limit your calling to the opportunities when it's most effective. If you're going to call, make sure you're in a good setup. And once you get into a good setup, have patience to stick with it. In fact, perhaps the hardest thing for a person to overcome in becoming a good caller is to have enough patience. For most of us, patience is something that has to be learned. For me, it certainly has been. And patience in elk country is something you have to learn in the context of elk country.

There's a common saying among hunters from back East: If you're a good white-tailed deer hunter, you'll be a good elk hunter, too. Somehow, that has never set right with me.

Chapter Four

ELK TACTICS

It paints the situation with too broad a brush. To me, such a statement would depend on what kind of whitetail hunting you do. If you do a lot of tree-stand hunting, you've gained one strength that a lot of western hunters don't have—you've learned to stay put in an area. But you probably haven't done a lot of stalking on the ground. A lot of elk hunting—some would say the majority of it—is moving quietly and stealthily on the ground. Ground hunting skills involve reading and recognizing situations that tree-stand hunters never encounter. It also involves playing the animals much differently.

It's about like saying a good pheasant hunter is going to be a good duck hunter. If all you've ever done is jump pheasants and they ask you to pass shoot at high-flying ducks, you'll understand how untrue this statement could be.

To me, a far truer statement would be that good elk hunters need to hone a wider variety of skills, some of which whitetail hunters undoubtedly have and some which they'll need to learn. Any hunter skilled in hunting a species, who pays attention to something new, is going to pick up the skills necessary for hunting another species much quicker.

If you live or spend time in elk country and have the opportunity to hunt elk for several years, you'll become a good elk hunter. And when you're dealing with problem elk, being a very good elk hunter is most important indeed.

CHAPTER FIVE

How to Make Elk Talk

There are some benefits to living in the heart of elk country. If you're an elk hunter, one of the biggest benefits is that you have a chance to be around elk both in and out of season. As an example, look no further than a recent winter morning on the banks of the Yellowstone River.

I was watching some elk—four cows and four calves—that were on the near bank of the river. The Yellowstone, at that spot, was running fast. But despite the swiftness of the current, four cows and three of the calves crossed the river to the far side without any trouble at all. But that last calf must have been a bit more unsure of itself than the others. It stayed on the near bank. And it was upset.

That calf repeatedly called across the river to the others. Its sounds were short, high-pitched calls. Typical of calves calling to their mothers, the elk's sounds were rapid. They were pleading. This calf was crying to its mother. After a period of time, the mother couldn't stand it anymore. She

ELK TACTICS

had been feeding on that far bank. But the calls of her calf finally got to her.

She got back into the water at that spot, with the flow so strong that the water was splashing over her back as she walked, and came back across the stream. It was a testament to these animals' power that she could withstand such a strong current and never lose a step. It was a testament to her mothering instincts that she came back.

As I stood there and watched, the other cows and calves eventually came back across the river, too, handling the current with relative ease. Together again, the four cows and calves found places to feed on the near side of the river and, after a time, I left them there.

The persistent pleading of that calf, however, stuck with me. I had heard the sounds often before as part of the repertoire of the many sounds that elk make. They were among the same sounds I've used to arouse the interest of cows myself. Calf sounds, back-to-back and plenty of them, will eventually bring elk toward you. They come to investigate. It arouses their curiosity. It creates a mood conducive to calling in elk.

Calf sounds, cow sounds, and bull sounds are all part of an elk hunter's bag of tricks. What do they all mean to an elk? That's hard to say, exactly. The pleading calls of a calf are pretty easy to interpret. But what about the occasional cow sounds you hear? What exactly are the bulls trying to tell us when they bugle back to our calls?

After so many years in elk country, I've got a theory or two about what the elk are saying. I know some sounds work all the time. Some sounds work part of the time. Some sounds tend not to work at all. It's knowing when to blow what sound that separates the consistently good callers from the hit-and-miss ones.

But I'll be the first to admit that I still can't speak Elk. I don't know what they're saying. All I know is what I hear, what I do, and how the elk have reacted to it over the years. Until we do learn to speak Elk or until the elk learn to speak English, we'll never know what all the variations

The science of determining a bull elk's size by his bugle is imprecise, at best, and sometimes you guess horribly wrong.

of elk language mean. But that won't stop us from trying, and learning, and becoming better at talking to elk.

Elk Sounds

You and I talk normal. But some of those people from other parts of the country—they talk a little weird. You can pick out a Southerner by his "y'all" and a Canadian by his "aboot, eh?" People say "youz" and "youse" for "you," "dem and dere" for "them and there," "Noo Yawk" for "New York," and "Bahston" for "Boston." There's even "aina" for "ain't that so." The bottom line is that people from different

Chapter Five

ELK TACTICS

parts of the country all talk a little differently—only you and I talk normal.

But from my experience, elk aren't like that. Over the years, I've called elk all over their range in the western U.S. I've found that elk are all pretty much the same animal. They have the same little drives and the same characteristics. And calling, from what I've seen and heard, is done exactly the same everywhere.

One time, I was down in Arizona, with a friend who had an elk tag there. I was along just to film the hunt. It came to pass that we worked our way into an area and saw some elk up a little canyon. All we saw were cows, but we decided to continue on anyway to see if there weren't some bulls up there with them.

We were hunting in the pre-rut. That's often a time when cow-calling is the most effective tactic. So we worked our way to a ridge above the elk, my friend lay down and I worked my way to a kneeling position so I could operate the camera. My friend cow-called once, and instantly one of the cows called back to him. To my ear, it was the same cow sound that cow elk back in Montana make. So my friend called back to her, imitating the sound.

That cow called back. And called back. And called back some more. That cow got so vocal that she kept answering and coming closer until she was not twenty-five yards from us. From that position, we talked back and forth for a half-hour. Finally, she left the area, still answering back to us every time we called to her. I got some great footage of it. It was the same trick I'd used for years in Montana. It was the same reaction to a cow call that cows have shown me in every state where I've called them.

Cow and calf sounds are pretty much universal, whether it's the higher-pitched chirp of a calf talking to its mother or the warning bark of a cow to alert the herd that something is wrong. For an elk hunter, that's a good thing. It means that you can use your cow-calling skills in the same way no matter where you wander in elk country.

I've found bull sounds to be the same, too. Elk in Arizona

and elk in Montana speak the same language, in the same way. But that doesn't mean that an elk's language is limited.

Take bull sounds, for example. There's a half-bugle, a full bugle, grunts only, a squeal, a high-pitched single note, a multiple note, a double bugle, a short bugle with grunts, a long bugle with grunts, a short bugle, a long bugle. Listen to the competitive callers; they make them all and do them in combinations. But as a hunter, do you need to make them all? My contention is that you do not.

If I had to pick out one bull sound to make, it would be the single, short, high-pitched squeal. And often, that's the only bull sound I make, for a couple of reasons. For one thing, the call is simple. It carries well. It's a sound for beginners and experienced callers alike, and it isn't going to give a real elk the chance to detect that I'm a fake. But there's another reason for using the single, short, high-pitched squeal.

One of the things I've noticed during my years in the field, both as a hunter and in filming elk and watching that film over and over later, is that the single, high-pitched squeal always seems to be the sound that bulls make when they're talking to cows. When I've made cow sounds to a bull, he's come back with that single, high-pitched note. When I switched to a bugle and made bull sounds, he's answered me with a bugle and some grunts. When a bull talks to other bulls, there are almost always those grunts at the end of their call.

That piece of knowledge can help you a lot when you're in the field. By listening to a bull's responses—and detecting whether he's moving in on you at the time—you can tell whether he's responding to your bull sounds or your cow sounds. Then you can adjust your calling accordingly to the sounds that are bringing the bull in most effectively.

The ability to tell the difference in a bull's reactions also gives you a clue as to how that bull is going to come in. When you bring a bull in with a bugle, they're often more alert and watchful in their approach. They're in a challenge situation, and the bulls seem to come in a bit more

Chapter Five

on edge, a little jumpier. If you bring them in with a cow call, they're not so alert. They're also more willing to stick with you a bit longer, allowing you to coax them in over a longer period of time.

Cow and calf sounds are universal, and all bull elk will respond to them.

The ability to hear who a bull's talking to has sometimes made it possible for me to change my calling strategy. I used to think that I always wanted the bull to be answering me. I thought that was a better situation, that when I bugled, he bugled. Now, I'll sometimes wait for the bull to bugle and then answer him with a cow call. If I can get him to respond to the cow call, instead of my bugle, it often takes only one or two cow calls to bring him in.

An example of how this can work: I was hunting once with a partner in Wyoming and we were working into an area where we had heard an elk bugle from a long distance away. I cow-called to the bull, and there was no answer. I cow called again, and the bull bugled back. We waited and waited for that bull to bugle again. When he did, I answered him with a cow call. After a bit, he bugled again and I answered him. That was all it took. The bull was on his way, and he came right in looking for that cow. We could have shot that bull with a bow and arrow. He was a six-point. But we were hunting for a trophy with a rifle and decided to pass.

Recognizing a high-pitched squeal as a bull trying to communicate with his cows goes against some common theories. Those high-pitched squeals are often thought to be the young bulls, the ones who haven't fully developed their voices yet. The bulls who make full bugles with grunts are thought to be the mature bulls. That common theory, however, has been proven wrong time and time again. The way it's often expressed is that you can't always tell a bull's size by its bugle. In the field, guys will hear a high-pitched squeal and think they're working on a young bull, then discover it's being made by a big bull. They'll hear a bugle with grunts and figure it's a big bull, then move in to discover the sounds are being made by a raghorn, or even a spike. It may just be—and I'm not professing to be an expert on this new theory, just a highly interested student—that what we're actually hearing is a difference in elk language by the same bulls, directed at other elk of a particular sex: squeals for the cows, and bugles and grunts for the bulls.

I've seen other evidence of this, too, and not just when I

Chapter Five

was using a cow call. When I make a high-pitched squeal, bulls often come right in after just one. I've had it happen with younger bulls and older bulls. I've always figured that this meant the bull was expecting a cow to be there somewhere nearby, perhaps a cow he could steal away from the bull who was squealing. It wasn't as intimidating to him as a full bugle and grunts would have been. To another elk, that full bugle and grunts is more of a challenge to fight. The squeal means a cow is there.

Anyone who has read *Elk Talk* or *The Elk Hunter* is familiar with my contention that cow and calf sounds should form the basis of any calling strategy. Those cow sounds can work for you in many ways. They'll locate elk bulls that squeal back or cows that talk to you. They can be used as a cover, to camouflage any sounds you may make as you move through the woods. And, of course, they can be used to actually call in elk.

Carrying it one step further, I also feel that pitch is an important ingredient in any cow or calf sounds you make. High-pitched sounds are better than low-pitched sounds.

Years ago, outdoor writer John Haviland was doing an article for *American Hunter* magazine on elk bugling in which he analyzed the bugles that bulls make. He interviewed me for that story, and we talked about the importance of those high-pitched sounds. In analyzing bull bugles on a computer, he found notes that were lower than the range of human bugles. I told him then that I felt the high notes were the key to sounding like an elk oneself. I still feel that way. These are the notes that an elk can hear, just as a dog hears one of those silent dog whistles.

Of the entire range of elk sounds we make, I truly believe that those high notes are the ones that are the most important to the elk. And it isn't just elk, either. I've been in correspondence with hunters from other parts of the world who have tried these calls on a variety of deer species. It turns out the "Cow Talk" call also works on roebuck. "Cow Talk" has been used successfully on red deer, on Asian elk, on sika deer, and on Japan's ezo shika deer.

In fact, one Japanese hunter wrote me that, in the first year he used the call on ezo shika deer, five of the six deer he took were with the call. The following year, it was ten of twelve deer. When you get a sound that works well on so many different species, there has to be a common denominator, and I've always figured that common denominator was the high-pitched sound.

Lending credence to the importance of the high-pitched sounds was a telephone call I received from an Oregon hunter soon after I came out with my Larynx Bull Call. The hunter said that he had called in a bull with a silent dog whistle and wondered if elk could hear in the higher frequency range. I told him that I had always had good luck calling elk with higher-pitched sounds, but I wasn't privy to any studies actually done on elk hearing—just what I'd found myself through experience. In the time since that phone call, we have found out that turkeys also respond to calls of very high pitch, as witnessed by the new turkey calls on the market that are producing sounds in the 15,000 hz. range and are working well. In analyzing elk sounds off recordings, the question has always been, "How good is the recording equipment?" All I can say for sure is what I've learned from my own hunting and filming experiences, and that has been that elk respond well to high-pitched sounds. Until somebody can prove to me that lower sounds work better, I am sticking to high-pitched sounds because I know they work, whether blown softly or loudly, depending on the circumstances.

With that in mind, it shouldn't come as much of a surprise that the bulk of my calling comes down to two basic sounds—the high-pitched squeal and a short, high-pitched cow sound. I don't limit myself to those sounds entirely. If an elk responds to a full bugle with grunts, then that's what I'll give him. If an elk wants me to match sounds with him, I'll do that. But first, and often last, it's those two sounds that form the vast majority of my calling.

Often, beginning callers will ask me for my recipe for calling, sort of a script they can follow so they know how to get started calling elk. Like any good recipe that a cook tinkers

Chapter Five

ELK TACTICS

with in his cooking, my calling recipe can be and is altered, depending on how the animal responds.

If I had to sum up my strategy for bull sounds, it would be squeals and single-note bugles in the pre-rut. In the rut, I'd use single-note and full bugles with some grunts. And during the post-rut, I would use strictly high-pitched squeals again.

But for just about all of my calling sequences, I'll start with cow sounds. I'll make one or two and make them pretty soft. I'll add more volume to my calling as I go along and try to reach out to elk that may be a distance away. That's one major modification I've made to my calling over the years. When I first began making cow talk, I thought you couldn't overdo it with loudness. Since then, I've compared my calling to fishing a pond. When you fish, your first casts are close to the bank for fish that may be nearby. Then, as you continue to fish, you keep casting farther and farther. When you do your cow sounds, you start out with soft sounds to cover the area around you. Elk have exceptional hearing. Those first soft sounds can sometimes be heard several hundred yards away. By the time you reach full loudness—and if sound conditions are just right to allow the sound to carry—you can literally pull elk in from a mile away, if you have the patience to wait for them.

When I was filming the video *Wyoming Thunder Bulls* with Murphy Love, we were working bulls that were very responsive to cow calls. Those bulls would bugle back to a cow sound almost immediately. So I'd make my cow sounds just loud enough so they could hear them. When the bull would bugle back, I'd answer him with a cow sound. It worked extremely well. I'd do one cow sound, then listen for two or three minutes before doing another cow sound. If a bull didn't answer, that didn't always mean a bull didn't hear me. We had a number of silent bulls move in on us and check us out without making a peep.

Another tactic that Murphy and I used on bulls that would respond with a bugle, but wouldn't come in, was to make cow sounds while staying mobile. When the bull bugled

The direction a bull is facing can sometimes fool you as to how close, or how far away, that bull might be.

back, we'd move on him. We'd call enough to figure out the direction the bull was moving and then work our way ahead of him, into his path. If you can accomplish that, you're bringing the bull in a direction he wants to go. He's much less likely to turn around and move off in a new direction. You can often bring him right in.

Invariably, when I tell beginners about high-pitched cow sounds and bull squeals being the basis of calling, they then ask me if those are the only sounds they need to know. And if they learn other sounds, when should they use them? The answer to that question is a bit tougher. The answer is that I'll do whatever works.

A number of times, I've called in bulls by answering their sounds almost identically. If a bull made a particular type of bugle, I'd make this bugle back. Of course, you can get carried away with this approach. One time, I was imitating a bull and had him coming in nicely. I finally got that bull up to within fifteen yards of me. And he was still bugling strong. So I figured I'd match him. I pointed the tube of my bugle right at him and let out the largest, loudest elk bugle I could make. He just looked right in my direction and gave me just as hard a bugle as he could bugle.

Chapter Five

ELK TACTICS

I thought for sure I'd spooked him out of there. But this time, it didn't faze him a bit. He held his ground. Other times, I've spooked bulls by bugling too loud when they were too close. It has literally blown them out of there. But as I said, whatever works.

Probably more important than anything is to call in elk country enough so that you can experiment with calling strategies of your own. Over time, each person develops his or her own style, based on what has worked in the past. That isn't to say it's going to work every time, but after a while you tend to sort out the things that will work for you. That's one of the reasons why the question was so tough about how many sounds a hunter really needs to learn. By learning a number of different elk sounds, you can sort them out for yourself. Remember that just as each elk caller has his own style, so does each elk.

It's in the blending of the two that you make your successes and failures. If your style works consistently for you, there's no reason for you to change what you're doing. But if you're not calling in elk on a regular basis, perhaps it's because some of your sounds or some of your calling sequences are wrong. That's when I'd advise you to go back to the basics of the high-pitched cow sounds and high-pitched squeals or, at least, to experiment with something new. Just keep calling and trying things until you hit on a method that works for you.

That degree of experimentation and learning is one of the things that has always fascinated me about calling elk. It's also one of the frustrations that many hunters are feeling over the new elk that they're facing in so many places today.

Old calling sequences and strategies that veteran hunters have been using for years may need to be changed. New theories and practices are developing now and, I suspect, will change again in the future. The wise hunter is one who isn't afraid to try something new. And, for the elk's part, don't be surprised if something new works. That, too, seems to be part of the nature of elk.

How else could you explain why bugles and cow calls

work in the first place? Think about it. You hunt your way into a group of elk that's got five, six, or seven bulls and countless cows scattered through an area. Yet when you blow your elk call, the elk come to you. What triggers that? There are other bulls bugling. There are other cows and calves talking. But the elk come to you. That's puzzled me for years. Yet the only theory I have to explain it is that these elk bugle and talk to each other twenty-four hours a day, and groups in fall may hold together for several weeks, at least. When I bugle and call, maybe they come in because I'm different and they feel the need to check me out. By that time, I'm sure they must know the voices of all the other elk in the group. We know that calf elk can identify their mothers by their voices and vice versa. Maybe all elk sound just enough different, to another elk, that they can tell each other by their voices. Certainly, people recognize individual voices and can tell others apart by them. Maybe elk can do the same. In any event, the sounds of my calls will attract elk. Maybe they think I'm the new bull in the mountains or a new cow looking to be bred.

Lending more ammunition to this theory is the fact that I've often returned to work the same bunch of elk a day or two later, tried the same thing, and the elk haven't responded to my calls. By that point, they've already heard you. They've checked you out. And if you've spooked them, or they've seen you, they seem to recognize your sound as something to avoid.

Once you sour elk with a call, they're most reluctant to respond again if they recognize your sounds. That, in turn, also puts a premium on having a number of sounds in your repertoire simply so you can try something different on them.

That being said, don't think that just because you may need to make different elk sounds that you need to line your pockets with every new elk call that comes out on the market. And this is advice coming from an elk call manufacturer, too. My own brand elk calls are the "Cow Talk" call, the "Larynx Bull Call," and the "Power Bugle." But there are others on the market that will make good sounds, too. The important thing is to find an elk call that you can blow eas-

Chapter Five

■ ELK TACTICS

Wallows are often in wet or marshy areas, but bulls will use ponds and rivers, as well, to cool off during the rut.

ily and gain confidence in and that makes good sounds. Those are the reasons I developed and sell these calls. But I'm not so bull-headed as to tell you that these are the only calls out there that will do these things. And I'm not so much of a blue-eyed optimist that I'm going to tell you that the next call to hit the market will be any better than the ones that already exist.

The truth of the matter is that manufacturers, even call manufacturers, come out with some new items every year. Some will be new and better. Some will be new and worse. Some will be just about the same as the ones on the market already. New products come out to generate new sales. When you actually get to calling animals, some of the best calls are the ones that were invented years and years ago. The critical thing is whether or not the calls make a good, clean sound that the animals respond to.

In fact, I sometimes think back to the first elk we ever called in with those old Herter's elk bugles. The call was pretty much just a straight tube that made a two-pitch whistle. In those days, we didn't even worry about anything like a grunt. And yet hunters took elk with them.

For a time, many of us made our own elk calls out of mountain squash, which we could find ourselves when we were out in the mountains. It was just a reed with some joints in it, hollow on the inside. We'd sit down and whittle a piece of wood with a flat spot on top and jam it into one end of the reed. Then we'd cut out a notch so it looked like a little flute. But when we blew it, it sounded something like a bull elk. It may not have been the best elk sound in the world, but it had a high pitch and it sounded enough like the right thing that the animals responded.

The thing to remember is that finding success with these old, old calls and many of the new ones comes down to more than being able to imitate every sound that an elk makes. Success still takes hunting skills beyond calling. It takes successful calling sequences and good, clean sounds. It takes more than having, in your possession, the latest elk call on the market.

In a nutshell, to me, calling comes down to basic sounds that you can make well. To start with, for me, those are cow sounds and the high-pitched squeal. From there, you try to read the bulls as well as you can, listening to how they answer you, and then answering them with what they want to hear, whether that's cow sounds, squeals, or full bugles and grunts. If the bulls want to be imitated, imitate them. If they want to hear a cow, sound like a cow. If you've got to move on a bull and get in its path to call him in, then head out and move. While calling undoubtedly works in a number of ways to bring elk within range, it's not so exacting a science that you can simply follow one recipe. So don't be afraid to experiment. And remember the experiments that were successful for you.

With the elk world changing as the animals react to increased hunting pressure, look for the science of elk sounds to continue to change and expand in the future as we gain more knowledge. But never forget, in the end, that you should do whatever works best for you.

Chapter Five

Seen and Unseen Elk

We've spent a lot of time talking about how important the setup is when you plan to call elk. We've talked about how you need to call from above, if you have any choice at all. We've talked about picking a spot that doesn't bury you in the timber. We've talked about moving into an area unseen. We've talked about the need for visibility, so that you can

When you can see the elk you're calling to, you can read its reactions to the sounds you're making.

see the elk once you get into your calling position.

The simple reason for this is that calling to elk you can see is far more productive than calling to unseen elk. Getting that view of an elk and seeing how the elk reacts to your calling gives you a giant leg up on the situation. To start with, you know absolutely that there's an elk out there in front of you. You also don't just hear how a bull reacts, you can see him. As a result, you can tailor your sounds to what the elk wants to hear.

While all elk may be the same critter, no matter what state you find them in, you have to remember that all elk are still individuals. They just react a bit differently. They all have their own little problems, and they're a product of their own experiences, too.

Some of that insight into elk has been gained since I started filming elk extensively a few years back. Instead of calling an elk in, shooting him, and then leaving elk country, filming gives you a good reason to come back and simply watch elk, seeing what they do and getting to know them on a more individual basis.

Over the past few years, I've kept track of one of the bulls that was hanging around our house in Gardiner. It was a spike, and he was distinctive. He tried to jump over a fence the first year I saw him, when his antlers were sixteen or eighteen inches high and were in the velvet stage. But when the bull jumped, he got his legs tangled and he went headfirst into the ground. The fall popped the skull plate on the spike and bent one of the antlers straight, so it stuck out about six inches beyond the end of his nose. It started to swell up. All that year, when the elk would try to feed, he couldn't get his nose down to the ground, because of the antler. Eventually, over a period of time, when he did eat he'd just eat the tops of the flowers and grasses. When he would drink, he would tip his head to the side. Eventually, that piece hanging past his nose broke off.

The damage done, however, continued. The pedicel on his skull, the place from which the antler grows, had actually cracked. It formed a big lump right there. So the next year, when he developed his antlers, the antler grew exactly

Chapter Five

ELK TACTICS

right and looked fairly normal, but grew down off the side of his face. That second year he became a bull with three points on one side and four on the other. But he managed to live with the deformity and thrive.

During that bull's third winter, he migrated with other elk and didn't come near my house. The last time I saw him, he was twenty miles below town and running with another bunch of elk. The winter migration seems to disperse them and makes them run with different animals. But the deformity from his youth continued. You could pick him out easily in a herd of elk. It made that bull an individual you could recognize. But, in truth, all bulls are individuals. And they all live their lives in certain ways.

One of the advantages to seeing the elk that you are calling is that you can make the most of that elk's individuality and not overcall. Over the years, I've found that the less I have to call, the better caller I become. Not everyone will agree with this. There are two schools of thought on calling. One school of thought is that a lot of calling will keep an elk's interest at a high level. But I've found that calling too much becomes an unnatural situation for some elk. Some elk don't like it. It will eventually scare some elk away. So instead, if I can monitor the situation by seeing the elk, I call just enough to keep the elk talking and answering. If that doesn't elicit a reaction, then I increase the frequency of my calling.

My eventual goal in calling is to arouse the curiosity of the elk, to make that animal want to come to me, to check me out. By not calling too loudly, I keep that curiosity alive. By not calling too often, I keep that curiosity alive. By being able to see the reactions of the elk to my call, I can keep the curiosity alive.

An example of how that can work was provided one day when I was filming some elk in the mountains near home. I was working toward an area where I wanted to do some calling, but had to skyline myself to do it. As soon as I reached the skyline, I saw the elk take off. It was a bunch of cows and calves, and the sight of me was enough to get them moving.

Understandably, I chastised myself. I figured I'd blown it. The elk were all gone. I should have been more stealthy. But rather than leave the area, I decided to sit down and take a break. I'd do some glassing to see what I could see. After a short time, a movement about two hundred yards away caught my eye. It turned out to be a deer. But as I watched the deer, I saw a cow elk slip through the trees and bed down.

With an elk in sight, it was worth attempting to call. If that cow was there, it was possible that other elk were nearby, too. As it turned out, the cow was alone. She was a young cow and didn't have a calf with her. But she taught me an interesting lesson anyway.

I set my camera up, focused it on where she was lying, and started the film rolling. I blew my cow call real softly—so softly that I thought perhaps she wouldn't even be able to hear it. The elk didn't move. At first, I figured she hadn't heard me. So I waited a couple of minutes, then I blew the call real softly again. At the sound, she jumped up quickly and ran about ten yards toward the sound. She didn't break out into the open, but stood there in timber near a tree and looked and listened. She had heard the first call, but didn't react. At the second call, she reacted strongly.

The advantage that I had in the situation was that I could see her. So when she looked away, appearing to lose interest, I blew the call again. This time, she answered me. She started calling and wanted me to answer her. I didn't give her that satisfaction. So she began to come closer, still looking for that elk she had heard. To my ear, I couldn't hear her calling. But when I got back to town, heard the results of my shotgun microphone, and looked at the film, she was calling all the way, making soft sounds through her nose.

The next time she stopped, she was about fifty yards away and was looking around. The wind conditions were perfect for me. She stood dead downwind. The setup was perfect, too. I was kneeling down, with a big rock and some sagebrush for cover. So I pointed the camera and just let the film roll. She called again. The cow kept looking around, throwing her head back and forth. When she looked in the oppo-

Chapter Five

ELK TACTICS

If a bull starts to turn away, or move in another direction, call again and you can turn him back your way.

site direction, I tried to make the sound she was making, a short, nasal sound similar to a deer sound.

When she heard the call, she whipped her head around and looked right at me. I didn't move. She started coming. And kept coming and coming until she was just ten yards away. At that point, she stopped looking straight at me and started looking around for the elk she knew must be somewhere nearby.

At about that time, I hit the point that all filmmakers dread. I glanced at my camera and saw that flashing light. My batteries were running out. I knew if I reached for it and started working on the camera, the cow would spook out of there. I needed her a bit farther away than she was, but didn't want to blow her out of the country. So I waved my hand just a bit. She caught the movement and ran back to fifty yards. Slowly, I changed the battery. Then I gave another cow call. Immediately, she answered and came to within twenty-five yards.

With no elk in sight and no movement from my direction, the cow must have figured she'd have to find the elk with her nose instead of her eyes, so she began making a circle. She passed out of view, making the 180-degree half-circle that would put her downwind of me. The next time I saw her, all I could see were her ears and eyes above the sagebrush. She was coming up behind me—the upwind side. She must have picked up a whiff of my scent because she barked a distress call and turned. I called to her and she turned back. Then she got a good whiff. This time, she ran off a longer distance before I stopped her with a call. From that point on, every time I made a sound, she barked. She barked and she barked and she barked. The cow finally went off through the trees and left the area, barking all the way.

Another example of calling to elk I could see was a time when I went on a trip with my friend Murphy Love to shoot some film.

The rut was just about over, but the bulls were still somewhat active. They could be called in to investigate, but wouldn't be coming to fight. It was another case where you wanted to heighten the curiosity of the elk, to make things

Chapter Five

interesting enough that they'd want to come in just to see what was going on.

Our plan was for Murphy to stay about two hundred yards behind me and use a bull call. We knew there was a bull there. So Murphy stayed back, out of sight, and I got into position on the side of a hill where I could stay low to the ground and see the elk. It was a case where I was the middle man. I would simply signal to Murphy when it was time for him to bugle.

When Murphy started his calling, the bull was so far away that it took a while for the sound to reach him. When it did, he raised his head, but didn't respond to it. The eight cows and four calves with the bull didn't respond either.

At the time, I was working on a new cow sound, using the Larynx Bull Calls with a new type of band. The band, part latex and part vinyl, made a very high-pitched call. It was a good cow sound, but of extremely high pitch. When the bull didn't respond to Murphy's calls, I figured I'd give the new band a try.

On my first call, the bull bugled back to me. I called again, and he bugled again. Every time I called, the bull would bugle. I think the bull was trying to call me in. He was making a short, high-pitched squeal that I'd heard often before when bulls were trying to communicate with cows.

At first, the cows and calves weren't too excited about the conversation between the bull and me. These elk were closer. But they weren't calling back at all. So, with the bull holding his ground and the cows and calves unresponsive, I switched sounds. I went to a more traditional cow sound—a short, soft sound with a bit lower pitch. Then I started stringing these cow sounds together, five or six of them in a row.

For whatever the reason, that long sequence tripped the trigger on one of the calves. The calf started answering and coming toward me. As I called again, the calf started running. A cow saw the calf running, and it started to follow. Then all the cows and calves started coming. Then the bull started coming. Interspersing these long series of cow calls with the high-pitched cow sound, I kept those elk on the move and answering. Before it was all over, I had that bull ten to fifteen yards from me, right below me, right out in the open. He would still bugle every time I cow-called.

The situation was a bit strange. I was out in the open, lying on my side on that hillside. I had no camouflage around me, no sagebrush or anything. All I had was netting around my camera and tripod so that the legs of the tripod wouldn't shine. Those elk were so curious about the source of those sounds, so engrossed, that they just wouldn't leave.

Finally, the calf that had been calling so much, and her mother, started up the hill. They worked their way up until they were right beside me, just scant yards away. With me staying low to the ground and not moving, they seemed unable to identify me as danger.

At the same time, two curious cows came from somewhere behind me. They were up on the ridge, looking down. By this time, I had to move around a bit, to reposition the camera. Those two elk behind me must have figured out what I was. Once that happened, the element of curiosity was gone. They must have signaled some kind of alarm because, all at once, all the elk started leaving. They never barked. They never ran. I know they didn't smell me. But whatever the element of curiosity was that I had built up to hold the elk there, all of a sudden it was gone. The cows and calves never responded again. They just walked away. As for the bull, he left, too, but he still kept bugling, every time I called with that one high-pitched band.

A similar type of situation occurred when I was out with Billy Hoppe; this situation also illustrates the advantages of being able to see elk and to react to what they do when they hear your calls. In this instance, it may have been hunting season, but Billy and I were just more or less goofing off. We didn't want to shoot an elk. We were just working on our calls and shooting some film.

This time, we spotted a little brush bull, a raghorn. He was a young bull, probably a two-year-old, and other than spikes, these are among the easiest of all the bulls to call in. They're also the bulls you often have the most fun with, just because they're so responsive.

Chapter Five

ELK TACTICS

Billy was using one of my "Cow Talk" calls, and he was going to do the calling. He got up on a hill about sixty or seventy yards above me, while I stayed down on a little bench with sagebrush around me, just for some cover. As we worked toward the spot, I sprayed some elk scent on the trail and into the air, because we had heard a bull bugling and thought he was over the hill. Then we heard this other bull and set up for him.

This second bull was perhaps seven hundred yards from us, down below, but we had the advantage of being able to see him just about everywhere he might go. He was coming from a direction where the wind would be in his favor before he'd get too close to us, so it was going to be a little tricky.

After I got set up, Billy began calling. And the bull was very responsive. He started running, and came up to an area about one hundred yards away, right to the spot where we had sprayed the elk scent. He never bugled. But the sound of our calls and the elk scent combined to hold his interest in that area. We worked the bull for twenty to twenty-five minutes. He'd come in, but not too close. When he started to leave, Billy would call and reel him back in. Finally, I pulled out a call and made a different sound. The bull turned around and started coming toward me in earnest. I honestly couldn't tell you exactly what made the difference. Perhaps it was the new sound. Perhaps it was a sound coming from a new position. All I can tell you is that the new sound made a difference. He came right in to my calling position and began making a circle around me, trying to see the elk making the new sound. As he made a half-circle around me, he was never more than thirty yards away, and was within twenty yards most of the time. Throughout this period, I was pretty much out in the open, low to the ground. He could see me. He certainly didn't know what I was.

Once he figured out that there wasn't an elk there and his curiosity was satisfied, he simply turned around and walked away. Since that time, I've looked at the film many times. That's one advantage of filming: You can go back and look at what you did, analyze what worked, analyze what didn't, and see how elk respond to the sounds you make. Often, a new sound, or a sound at just the right time, makes all the difference in the world. It literally turns a situation that could have gone sour into a huge success story. It has also convinced me that, if at all possible, you should get into a posi-

When you're calling to an unseen elk, you have to imagine what the elk looks like and how he's reacting to your calls.

Chapter Five

ELK TACTICS

tion where you can see the animal that you're calling. If you can see the elk, and see how he or she responds, it makes a huge difference.

Of course, that's a luxury that isn't always possible in elk country. Like it or not, we're often calling blind. And with silent elk, we're not just calling blind, but we're calling deaf, too. That's the worst of all worlds, but it's a world you often face.

I've always divided blind calling into two types. One type is when you have no idea if there's an animal in the area or not. The other type is when you've got a pretty good idea that an elk is there, based on a sound you heard or tracks, but you aren't quite sure where the animal is holding. Basically, however, the approach to the two types is the same.

In all blind calling, I like to take things slowly and carefully. I'll try to pick a good setup, just in case an elk is nearby, a place where I can see for a distance. Then, I'll sit there for a while quietly and try to take in all the sights and sounds around me. Is there a squirrel, or a jay, or a raven scolding something that might be an elk? Are there any sounds of elk, whether those sounds are bugles, or brush breaking, or a branch snapping? Take in all the sounds, do a little glassing, take your time. There's no rush to haul out the call and start blowing.

When I do start to call, I use just one cow sound, not too loud. Then I'll wait five or ten minutes. Then I'll move anywhere from fifteen to twenty yards, set up in another position where I can see well, and I'll blow a couple of cow sounds. These sounds are just a bit louder. Then I'll wait some more, even longer than I waited the first time.

What you have to remember is that you are trying to call to an elk, even if you don't know whether there's an elk there or not. That requires patience. You may have an elk that's fairly close that has heard your first call, but hasn't decided whether or not to respond to it. By the time you do your second calls, that elk may be making up his mind. Even if the elk doesn't answer back, the elk has heard you. They can hear for a long, long way. They have keen hearing, and their ears are large.

After that second series of calls, I'll often sit there for fifteen or twenty minutes. It often takes that long for an elk's curiosity to be aroused and for it to come in. All that time, it may never make a sound. But all too often, a hunter fails to wait the elk out. I can't tell you how many times a person has moved from his calling spot and then bumped the animal that's coming in. Once bumped, it's a lot more difficult to turn the animal around.

After the fifteen- to twenty-minute wait, do another single cow call. Then wait again. If after a time, you're convinced no elk has heard you, or that no elk is responding, it's time to move on and look for another place to call.

Believe me, describing this calling sequence is much easier than actually pulling it off. What it means is that you've basically stayed in one spot for somewhere between a half-hour and an hour, with absolutely no sounds coming back to you and no sign that there's an elk in the country. Yet that's what you have to do, and if you do it religiously, one of those times you're going to be surprised by turning around and seeing a silent bull looking at you, or hearing a bull bugle from somewhere so close it will make the hair on the back of your neck stand on end.

It's important throughout this calling sequence to keep a low profile. That doesn't mean you can't move a bit, put up your binoculars, and glass the timber or the clearings below. A little movement isn't going to make a huge difference. But walking around, talking, scuffing your feet, or any huge movements are definitely discouraged. Those movements can blow a situation.

Also, don't underestimate the importance of glassing with a good pair of binoculars when you're calling blind. To me, it always seems to be an odd angle or a particular color that gives elk away. The angle of an elk's ears is something that's engraved in your mind, after you've seen a lot of elk. There's the color of antlers that can tip you off. It can be the off-color of an elk's legs. I can remember once when I looked far up a mountain slope in the gloom of pre-dawn and noticed that there were some funny-colored sticks up

Chapter Five

ELK TACTICS

there. When I pulled out my binoculars, it turned out that those funny-colored sticks were actually elk legs, catching the first light of day. There were more than twenty elk in the group, but with the naked eye in that poor light, all I could see was something that looked like funny-colored sticks.

Often, elk that come in quietly will stand there for a long period of time, looking over the situation without moving a muscle. It's easy to spot an elk when he flicks an ear or turns his head, but to spot a motionless elk, or a part of a motionless elk, in the timber requires a real close look. But if you have the patience to wait them out, or to spot them standing there, you can bring those elk in.

Calling blind can also produce some strange results. I had a good friend who was an outfitter and was guiding a hunter once. He was having some difficulty locating them, because the elk weren't making any noise. On this particular day, it was getting toward noon, but the outfitter wanted to check out a lot of country and figured he could check it out quicker on his own than he could with the hunter in tow.

So they tied up the horses, and the outfitter told this hunter to take a break, eat his lunch by this tree, and to wait there while the outfitter made a big swing to cover some country. He left the hunter there by the tree. But, after a lunch and a wait, the hunter got kind of bored.

The hunter had one of my cow calls. So he figured he'd practice with it for a while. He sat by the tree, blowing his call. Admittedly, the hunter's intent wasn't to call in an elk. He was simply killing time, waiting for the outfitter to come back. He blew the call for a while. Then he leaned his gun up against a tree. He watched his horse, tied to a nearby tree. He thought about taking a nap.

Then he'd blow the cow call a few more times. He'd blow it one way. Then he'd tighten the band and try it again. He'd loosen the band and try it again. This went on for about a half-hour. When it was all over, he looked up, and there, about forty yards away, stood a six-point bull looking at him through the timber. The hunter was sitting with his back against a tree, so he reached around and

Bugling bull elk fill the mountains with elk music in the month of September.

grabbed his rifle and had a perfect shot at forty yards. He nailed the six-point.

The outfitter told me that he heard the shot and became concerned about what the shot might have been. He thought maybe someone else was in the area. Maybe his hunter's gun misfired. Who knows? In any event, the outfitter was quite a distance away, but he immediately headed back to the tree where he'd left the hunter.

When the outfitter got there, he saw the bull and the smile

on the hunter's face. As it turned out, it was the largest six-point taken in that hunting camp all season.

What's the lesson in this little tale? You figure it out. The hunter wasn't following any set sequence. He wasn't even necessarily making all good sounds. He wasn't really attempting to call an elk, though he was in an excellent spot. And somewhere in the middle of calling all those different ways, he'd attracted a very nice six-point bull.

If there's a nugget of wisdom in all of this, it may be that in the midst of all his calling, the hunter must have been making some good elk sounds. He certainly stuck with it. He exercised the greatest of patience, as he waited and waited by that tree. And, of course, he found a bull that was responsive to coming in to a call.

For the hunter's part, he couldn't have been happier. He had called in a six-point bull all by himself. As for the big bull, he must have died confused. All he heard were these strange elk noises, apparently coming from that horse tied to a tree.

Call a Little, Call a Lot

Competition elk callers do put on quite a show. They come on stage with a variety of paraphernalia. They often have several calls, tubes of several sizes, and an extension or two on the end of those tubes. Then they stand there and go through their routine. They make cow and calf sounds, loud ones and soft ones. They point their tubes in various directions to spread the sound around. And they make a wide variety of bull sounds.

If you're judging one of these competitions—and I've judged a number of them from the local level to nationals a couple of times—you can't help but be impressed with the show. You're hidden behind a screen, so you can't see the paraphernalia and the gyrations these folks go through. But you're sitting in the best of places to hear them. The good callers make themselves sound like a whole herd of elk of all sizes, ages, and sexes. From the sound of it, you could

Given the choice between making a lot of sounds, or just a few, my preference is to be sparse in my calling.

swear there were a dozen or more elk out there. Their sounds are that good. They put on a hell of a show.

But how does that competition calling parlay into actually calling in an elk? I'll be honest. From my experience, the

Chapter Five

link between the quantity and variety of sounds you make in competition and the sounds you make in the field is a tenuous one. In fact, I'm not sure it exists at all. For sure, no elk hunter could carry all the paraphernalia into elk country that these guys carry onto the stage. But I doubt whether they'd even want to make all those sounds. I don't mean to sound condescending toward these callers. Most often, these callers are good elk hunters, too. They make good sounds in the field. They often possess the good hunting skills. But I can't help but believe that, in their actual hunting, they leave most of their elk sounds back on the competitive stage.

The only reason I mention this is because I've watched and heard too many novice callers come away from one of those competitions with the wrong perspective on calling. Those with this perspective tend to fall into two groups. One group thinks that they have to learn and do all those things themselves, or they'll never call in an elk. The other group is even more fatalistic—they flat believe they can't learn those things, so they won't even try.

What I've tried to get across in the pages of this book is that calling shouldn't be a formidable obstacle to a hunter. It isn't a silver bullet, either, that will guarantee you an elk, just because you toot on a call. Instead, calling should be just be viewed as one of the tactics that a hunter has at his or her disposal. Calling can revolve around making just a few different sounds—and making them well—especially if you're just a novice caller. It's also a skill that can grow with you, and that you can have fun with, as you become a veteran elk hunter.

One of the questions that hunters are left with, especially after viewing an elk-calling competition, is how much should they call. Should you call a little? Should you call a lot? Unfortunately, the answer isn't so cut and dried, though we all develop our own preferences.

I talked once with a hunter from Oregon, who had been using the "Cow Talk" call since it had come on the market. He told me that he had gotten an elk by using the call every year. The hunter said his strategy was something he referred to as constant calling. He'd work into prime elk areas, start making cow sounds, and just keep making those sounds. Eventually, sticking with that strategy, an elk would come in. It was the system that worked best for him.

I've talked to others who have used similar systems. One of the terms being used for it is double-calling, or rolling the sounds, or making lonesome cow sounds, or aggressive cow calling. Whatever you call it, the system involves repeated, multiple calls. Sometimes the caller will drag the sound out, or put a high pitch to it. At times, this type of calling can charge elk up. If elk are receptive to it, it seems to get their juices flowing. In a way, it's almost like a distress sound for elk, an animal that's bothered and just won't shut up. Doing it this way, you're going to be making a lot of noise. Receptive elk aren't going to be able to ignore you forever.

There are examples from real life when elk do just this. One time, I had some elk near my house, on the outskirts of Gardiner. In that bunch of elk was a calf that was looking for its mother. The calf was calling to her nonstop. Finally a cow answered, and the calf ran over to it and smelled, but realized it wasn't its mother. So the calf continued calling and moved on, from cow to cow. The sound the calf was making was a short, high-pitched sound.

When a cow answers her calf, she answers it in two ways. One way is a long, drawn-out sound, and if you watch the cow do it, she'll roll her tongue. The sound becomes a lot longer than a normal cow sound. Normally, when a cow is calling her calf, she opens her mouth wide and it's a fairly loud sound. But when cows are talking among themselves, they normally don't open their mouths. They make the sound through their noses.

This calf called and called, and the other elk in the yard feeding never responded. Only the one cow did, and the calf ran up to it. The rest of the elk could care less. The calf went right through the herd and on down the country, looking for its mother. It never stopped calling—like a baby crying for attention, all the way out of sight.

To my mind, there's little doubt that elk can identify each other by their sound, even if this cow-calf incident shows otherwise. I'm sure they all make their own individual sounds, just like humans do. To us, they sound alike. To them, we probably sound alike.

It's pretty interesting when you get a group of elk moving. You can hear the old cow sound as she calls her calf. You can hear a lot of calf sounds, as they call to locate their mothers. When elk are moving, they're very vocal, especially in the morning when they're leaving their feeding grounds. Or if they're getting close to their bedding area. Or if somebody disturbs them.

The two theories on calling reflect those sounds of elk moving, or of a lone animal. The first is doing a lot of sounds, very similar to predator calling, where you do distress sounds constantly. Or the simple method, which is doing short sounds and spacing them out.

My preference has always been the latter. I don't use as many sounds, especially if I don't have an elk within view so that I can read its reactions. My system would be to make sounds much more sparsely. That works for me.

There have been times when I've used a blending of the two systems. I've used the sparse calling to locate elk and bring them in. Then, if I've had other hunters with me, I've had them join in with some cow calling. By having more than one caller, you invariably increase the frequency of the calling. By having the sounds come from more than one spot, you also give the impression that there is more than one elk in the area.

The "Cow Talk" call, which is a bite-and-blow call that I manufacture, offers another option for multiple cow and calf sounds by allowing you to adjust the rubber band at each end. I'll make one end tighter to give it a higher-pitched tone for calf sounds. I'll loosen the band at the other end of the call, giving it a lower-pitched tone for cow sounds. Other types of calls may give you other options for varying the tone of the call. Or you can choose to carry several different kinds of calls along. At times, that can be the difference in exciting an elk enough to come in to a call. Other times, it doesn't seem to matter that much. It's

A bugling bull won't make the wide range of sounds, or the long calls, that you're likely to hear at an elk-calling competition.

something to remember and is worth a try.

One of the things that has always surprised me is that, whether you make cow sounds, calf sounds, or a combination of them, even when you make only a few calls, the elk have no trouble pinpointing exactly where you're calling from. Their hearing must be exceptional. Their ability to zero in on the source of that sound is equally amazing.

I remember an occasion when a friend and I were working some bulls. We'd done the shooter-and-caller setup, with the shooter placed about seventy-five yards in front of the caller. We were doing this in the timber, and I could just barely see where the friend was out there.

From that position, as the setup progressed, the friend made just a call or two, and the sounds he was making were different than the bugling and cow calling that I was doing. As we worked a bull, the friend decided that the bull was coming in on a slightly different path than we expected. The

Chapter Five

ELK TACTICS

bull was coming in higher on the slope than where my friend was positioned. So the friend left the spot where he had been calling and quietly slipped up the slope a distance and set up again, but didn't call.

What the friend didn't know was that the bull was actually coming straight in on him, apparently homing in on those few cow sounds he had made. But each time the bull bugled, he must have been turning his head in different directions. By throwing his sound off that way, it disguised the bull's truth path.

The end result was that moving up the slope backfired on the hunter. The bull came straight in. In fact, he homed in on my friend's few cow calls so strongly that if he had stayed in his original setup, that bull would have presented him with about a ten-foot shot. As it was, from his new position, he had no shot at all.

Rather than beat ourselves up for it, the friend and I had a good laugh over the incident. We remarked about how smart we were—and how we had actually outsmarted ourselves. But, in retrospect, that's some of the fun in calling. You try to outsmart the elk. Sometimes they outsmart you. Then you get to go and try it all over again.

Another time, I was hunting with another friend in the Bull Mountains of Montana, and we were working two bulls that had been bugling in another canyon. They were so far away that we weren't sure if they were calling to each other, to other elk, or were responding to our calls. We listened to them bugle, then sat there for thirty minutes, waiting to see if they were moving on us.

After such a long time with no action, we figured to drop down into the timber and get a bit closer. But about the time I stood up, I looked over my shoulder just in time to see one of the bulls coming in. Unfortunately, he spotted me at the same time. The hunt for that bull was over.

One of the things to remember, especially with calling a little, but even with calling a lot, is that these elk are going to come in at their own speed. I've had them come at a dead run, literally coming to a skidding halt just a few yards

Elk have no difficulty in pinpointing the source of a sound, then moving in directly toward that source.

away. I've also had them come in so painfully slow that I didn't think they were coming at all. They'd come a little ways, take a bite or two of grass, walk a little, feed a little, and eventually work their way to a point scant yards from where I was calling.

It's almost impossible to predict which way an elk is going to react. It's also impossible to tell when, where, and if an elk is going to respond.

Chapter Five

I've talked to a lot of hunters who have told me about their great success with calling on opening days of the season. That's understandable, to a point, because elk haven't been called yet that year, and elk won't be call-wise on opening day. Those hunters have called elk in with a little bit of calling, or a lot of calling.

I've talked to a lot of first-time callers, too, who have gone out and had success with their calls the first season they use them. Sometimes success came at the start of the season, and sometimes it was well into the course of the hunting season. That's understandable, to a point, as well. First-time callers who put in the time to practice their sounds in preseason are more likely to keep their calling sweet and simple, making just a few good cow and bull sounds and sticking to them rather than adding the sour notes that sometimes accompany more complicated bugles.

What's going to work best for you? We've presented a lot of options here, from calling a little to calling a lot, and from having just one caller to having several callers, and from using just cow sounds to using just bull sounds to using a mixture of both.

Each of these calling strategies has accounted for elk being taken by hunters. Each one will work at some point in time. I can tell you the system I prefer—and I have. But I'm not going to be so presumptuous as to tell you which will work best for you. You've simply got to go out and try them. Develop your own style. Remember the tactics that work for you. Keep using them as long as they work. If they don't work, then don't be afraid to move on and try some other systems.

If you're a good student of elk calling, and a good student of elk hunting, you'll add to your own knowledge this way and help the rest of us learn a little more about calling and hunting, too.

CHAPTER SIX

Gearing Up

Imagine if you had an unlimited checkbook. Imagine if cost was no object. You could walk into any sporting goods store you chose and outfit yourself with all the best things you could find. You could get one of those outdoor catalogs in the mail and make a long list of clothing and equipment—and then order it without fear. Unfortunately, that's just a dream for all but a small handful of us elk hunters. Instead, we have to plan our purchases wisely. We have to budget our purchases carefully. We build our stash of gear season after season, until we get most—but surprisingly never all—of the things we want.

For that reason, it's important that you make your purchases wisely. There are tons of things out there that are marketed for elk hunting. If you read the advertising on them, you'd think they all were perfect for just what you want. Unfortunately, however, some of the advertising doesn't match up with what you really need.

ELK TACTICS

In this section of the book, what you're going to get is some guidance—no more, no less, just guidance—about some of the things you may want to purchase for elk hunting. In some of the items we're talking about, you're going to hear my biases for them, or against them. That doesn't mean my biases are any better than yours, or that you might not like some other product better. If you really like something, stick to it. I'll certainly stick to what I like. But if what you're using has some shortcomings, recognize them and perhaps find something better.

One of the things you won't read about in this section are elk calls. I've made mention of the calls I manufacture in other parts of this book. I'm not going to beat you over the head with the notion that they're absolutely better than any other calls on the market. They work for me, and they've worked for others. Enough said. Instead, this book is aimed at the strategies and tactics you need, no matter what brand of calls you're using. So rather than try to impress you with some kind of testimonial, we'll talk about other things you may need.

The things we are going to talk about here are not all items you absolutely need right away. You don't have to run out and purchase them right off the bat, or feel that you can't hunt without them. One of the things most hunters have learned over the years is making do with what they have and not blowing the family budget in the process. And if you're tempted to blow the family budget, remember that no matter how much you love the sport, elk hunting is recreation. Recreation should always come in a distant second behind family needs and family responsibilities. Hunters who violate that ethic—who spend freely on themselves while the rest of the family suffers—have never commanded my respect or the respect of other hunters, no matter how many elk they may stack up. Family first, foremost, and always.

The items described in this section are things you can gather as you need them, and as your budget allows. In time, with good purchases of well-made equipment, you'll acquire all the things you desire. In some ways, you already have the things you absolutely need—a level of knowledge, a desire to learn more, a motivation to pursue elk, a will to succeed. Past that, everything is just one more piece of equipment.

Rifles and Bows

Let the arguments begin!

It doesn't really matter much what I write in this section. It's going to get me in trouble with somebody. And maybe it will get me in trouble with everybody.

Few arguments are fought as fervently in hunting camp as what type of weaponry a hunter chooses to use. And few questions have less hard and fast answers, either.

Whether you're talking about rifle calibers, types of rifle actions, bow weights, or bow types, it all comes down to a matter of personal preference.

I've had rifle hunting partners who've talked about .348 magnums with the types of terms that really should have been reserved for their wives. I've heard glowing reports about .270s that made them sound as if all they shot were silver bullets.

But in all honesty, I really don't care much what caliber you shoot. There are a lot of calibers that are good for elk. Among the calibers I'd list as good elk rounds are the .270, .280, .30-06, .308, 7 mm., 7mm. Remington magnum, .300 Winchester magnum, and .348 Winchester magnum. Those seem to be the calibers that most hunters are choosing.

What has always been more important to me is how they're shooting them. If you're comfortable with a rifle and shoot it accurately, that's the rifle you want to use. If you're not comfortable with a rifle and don't shoot it well, then it's time to find a rifle you can shoot. Far more important than the size of the caliber is your ability to place a shot accurately.

In truth, that's the problem I have with some of the bigger magnum calibers. While they send a bigger bullet at tough game—and elk are tough—too often the shooters can't handle the caliber and shoot them poorly. They get punished at the bench rest, sighting them in. They get punished

Chapter Six

■ *ELK TACTICS* ▬▬▬▬▬▬▬▬▬▬▬▬▬▬▬▬▬

Rifle hunters shouldn't just think about the caliber, but should be very choosy with their choice of a bullet for elk.

in the field when they're forced to shoot at odd angles and in uncomfortable positions. Sometimes, shooters develop bad habits when these things happen. Sometimes, they flinch. Sometimes, they miss elk or, even worse, place a shot in the elk poorly.

Does that mean big magnums are bad? No, not if you can handle them. But if you can't handle them, they are bad for you. Then it's time to back off to the .270s, .280s, .308s, and .30-06s. The bullets they deliver—even the 130-grain rounds of the .270—are big enough and powerful enough to do the job on an elk, and the bullet placement for the average shooter is often much better.

That said, let me add that perhaps more critical than the rifle caliber you choose for elk is the type of bullets you choose to put through the barrel. Your killing power, your knock-down power on game, depends a tremendous amount on how the bullet performs. You may have a caliber big enough to knock down an elephant, but if the bullet doesn't perform correctly, it doesn't do any good.

Too often, shooters choose jacketed bullets that never open up. They're so tight that they're through the animal before the bullet mushrooms. Other times, reloaders will put together a round with a light bullet that's so fast, the bullet breaks up when it enters the animal and doesn't hold together at all. In either case, you're not going to get much killing power out of your bullet. Ideally, you want a bullet that mushrooms and holds together, delivering all its power in the animal, then barely cuts the hide on the opposite side.

For me, the best bullet performance I ever had was a .270 round with a 130-grain, lead-core bullet. The only problem with it was that the nose of these bullets had a tendency to deform when they were stored in the rifle's magazine. Since then, I've gotten about the same performance, and no deformed bullet noses, with the Nosler Ballistic Tip. But, certainly, that's not the only good bullet around. The important thing is to analyze the performance of the bullets you do use, not just in their groups on paper, but in how they work on game.

As far as rifle actions are concerned, I'm a dyed-in-the-wool bolt action man. They're not the fastest action, but they've more than proven their accuracy over the years.

And when I hunt these days, I always use cross-sticks. Cross-sticks seemed to fall out of favor a number of years ago. Most people just got away from using them.

One friend of mine, Al Lee, however, was among those who kept the faith in his sticks over the years. Al grew up hunting antelope and deer in open country and knew the value of a steady, solid rest that you carried along yourself, because the open prairie offered few rests of its own.

These days, he does most of his cross-stick shooting with

Chapter Six

ELK TACTICS

old buffalo rounds and shoots competitively out to one thousand yards off those sticks. While he'd be the first to tell you that there are better shots than he is, I've watched him perform off those sticks. And I'm not the one who's going to challenge him to a match.

These days, some companies are bringing out models of cross-sticks commercially, and they're enjoying something of a rebirth. Or you can make some of your own out of wood dowels with a leather thong for a hinge.

Bipods, which attach to your rifle, are also available, but you've got to get the more expensive models that allow you to rock your rifle back and forth to make sure you've got your crosshairs straight up and down. Some bipods are fixed, and you've got to adjust the length of the legs to get the crosshairs straight. Then, if the animal moves, you've got to adjust the legs again and hope the animal doesn't move a second time.

With either cross-sticks or bipods, you can improve your shooting accuracy immensely. With antelope, which provide a small, small target out on the prairie, sons Andy and Matt have pulled off one-shot kills at ranges greater than four hundred yards. And son Ryan and daughter Lori made equally impressive shots at similar ranges on mule deer by using cross-sticks.

If you can hit antelope and deer with them at those ranges, imagine the confidence-builder they can be with an elk-size target at closer distances.

Which brings us to archery hunting.

Here, too, you're asking for arguments as soon as you start picking one type of bow over another or one type of arrow instead of the next.

I can tell you that, over the years, I've tried every type of bow from a long bow to a recurve to compounds of varying descriptions. I've tried sights and no sights. I've used gloves and releases. And I've taken more than a few elk with a bow, too, including some very nice bulls.

I've used bow weights as heavy as ninety pounds. I've used full-length arrows. I've used overdraws. I've tried my

For bowhunters, arrow placement is everything, and you need an elk to show you a good angle for the shot, too.

luck with sharpen-'em-yourself, old-style broadheads and razor inserts, too—two-blades, three-blades, and four-blades. And some of the archery equipment I haven't used myself, I've seen in the hands of my friends in hunting camp.

From what I've used and what I've seen, the most important facets of bowhunting for elk are the same ones that are important for rifle hunters. A bowhunter has to be able to place his arrows accurately if he wants to bring down an elk, no matter what kind of equipment he's using. For that reason, the best bowhunters are invariably the ones who spend the most time on the practice range.

The strength of your bow, like the size of a rifle caliber, is a matter of how well you can handle it. A 90-pound bow is a good weapon, if you have the strength to hold it back while you wait for an elk to turn his head or emerge from behind a tree. If you don't have the strength, I've seen bows in the 65-to-70-pound range that drilled an elk very nicely and were much easier to hold at full draw for longer periods of time.

Once you have your accuracy, the next most important ingredient is the type of broadheads you use. Most of the broadheads on the market today are being designed for deer hunters, with elk as a distant secondary market. As a result,

Chapter Six

the razor inserts and broadhead points are of relatively thin gauge metal. I've seen some blades break when they hit an elk bone. I've seen the points of broadheads bend badly.

What you're looking for in an elk broadhead is strength. Look to the razor insert heads with the heavier gauge metal. Look to the broadheads that are beefier in construction, too.

There's a large cult of bowhunters who firmly believe in those old-fashioned sharpen-'em-yourself, one-piece broadheads simply because those heads are so strong. I can remember one of those heads: It penetrated the front of an elk full-length, going up through the chest of the animal, then buried itself completely in the bull's spine, but looked untouched when I removed it. That's the type of strength you're looking for in an elk broadhead.

No matter what type of head you use, make sure that it's sharp. Elk hide is much thicker than the hide of a deer or antelope. You want the head to slice through it easily. That means, if you're using razor inserts, you need to put in fresh blades after you've sighted in your bow. If you're using one-piece heads, make sure they're absolutely sharp.

I've heard pluses and minuses about using sights on bows. Some hunters swear by them, saying they help an archer achieve pinpoint accuracy. I've heard some hunters swear at them, too, because many sights are almost useless in the low-light situations of dawn, dusk, and dark timber because you can't see through the peep or can't see your pins. If you do use a peep sight on your string, make sure it's drilled out to allow more light through it. If you use pins, paint them bright colors so they stand out in low light or try the new fiber-optic pins for low-light situations.

As to whether you should use heavy, full-length arrows or light, short arrows for an overdraw, it's a matter of personal preference as far as I'm concerned. I've killed bulls with both. With the heavy, full-length arrows, your arrow is slower and you have to adjust your sights higher for longer shots, but you get better penetrating power. With the short, light, fast arrows, you rely on speed for penetration, but different distances don't affect your point of aim as much.

The important thing remains, if you're a bowhunter, you need to be able to put an arrow exactly where you want it to go. And if you're a rifle hunter, you've got to be able to place your bullet just right.

That puts a premium on practice before you get into elk country. It means you have to be realistic about range when you shoot and not take shots at distances beyond your ability. And it means all the arguments in the world don't mean a thing if you can't take your rifle or your bow and shoot well with it.

Clothing and Camo

Someday, I'm going to find the perfect hunting clothes. At least, I really hope I do. Because, frankly, right now I'm dressing myself in compromises, and those compromises are filling up my closets.

I've got warmer-weather hunting clothes. I've got middle-weather hunting clothes. I've got cold-weather hunting clothes. I've got boots for different seasons. My camouflage situation is even worse—but more on that later.

When you outfit yourself with clothing for elk hunting, you have to ask yourself some questions. What type of terrain am I going to be hunting? What is the weather likely to be? How much is that weather going to change? What do I really need?

In the high country of Montana where I do most of my elk hunting, these questions are likely to produce a wide range of answers. In early September, when bowhunting season begins in my home state, there are afternoons when the temperature may climb into the seventies and eighties. By January, when the late rifle hunts are on, it could be far below zero. In between, you've got equinox storms that blow into the high country and turn sunny skies, bare ground, and a warm afternoon into an icebox with deep snow and a howling wind by the following morning. You've got the more steady onslaught of winter, which can

Chapter Six

Hunters have to be able to move through elk country quietly, not tipping off elk with loud boots or rough fabrics.

gradually do the same thing. And you've got varying weather all along the way.

So what do you need for clothing?

To start with, the primary requirements for elk hunting clothes are that they be warm and quiet and, if possible, offer some degree of water repellency. That's a tough mixture to attain. Water repellency, especially, tends to make most fabrics hard and noisy—that's bad for elk hunting. But if you go for warmth and quiet, the fabrics often don't have water repellency or wind-breaking ability. Only the most expensive clothes seem to offer a degree of everything, and you're still going to find some of them lacking in certain respects.

If I had to choose which ingredients were most important for clothing that I wear most of the time when I'm elk hunting, it would be quiet and warmth. For this, you still can't beat wool, and I'd rank some fleece products as a pretty-close second. What that means, however, is that you'll have to bring something extra along to wear over the top or underneath for the days when it's raining, snowing, or extremely windy. In fact, I can remember one rain-spattered day when I shot a darn nice bull while I was wearing a gray, rubberized raincoat over my fleece.

Boots present a similar problem. If there's a single boot made that covers all situations, I have yet to find it. Here again, however, the key requirements are warmth and quiet.

I've got horror stories in my past about hunting with others who wore hard-soled, rugged-tread boots. Even with my hearing, I could hear them scuff their feet on hard trails. I've heard the clunk of those boots on rocks. I've heard them bang against downed timber. A hunter's ability to move with stealth through elk country is, in large measure, a matter of his footwear. It's something you've got to choose carefully.

Now I've seen and heard some people who have carried this to the extreme. I've seen hunters out in the forest with flimsy, soft-soled, canvas sneakers on. While I applauded their zeal in trying to be quiet, I could only shake my head at the notion of hiking all day with no ankle support and no protection for the sides of my feet from wayward rocks. I've heard about guys who carried it one step further, too, and took off their boots when they stalked so they could move more quietly. But I sometimes hunt elk country that has cactus in it. Everywhere I go, there are sharp-edged rocks. And I think more of my feet than to beat them up that way.

With that in mind, in the old days, I thought that crepe

Chapter Six

ELK TACTICS

rubber, wedge soles were just about as good as it got. They were very quiet. But they were a bit slippery. If you used them all the time, however, you learned how to walk with them and get by in most situations without losing your footing. From there, I went to the air bob soles, which offered similar quiet walking, but added much better traction for climbing around in the mountains. The other quiet sole for walking was, and still is, the gum rubber bottoms of the L.L. Bean pacs, with the rubber soles and leather uppers. These have a chain link tread on the soles which, unfortunately, wears out fairly quickly with hard use in rocky terrain, but is very quiet for walking and stalking.

Another consideration for elk hunting boots is that they provide good ankle support. That means you're going to want tall boots, with good quality leather, so that you can cinch them up tight. Those boots are going to be heavier than the short hiking boots, but the added support will make the extra weight worthwhile.

All of these boots are still good choices. And there are some manufacturers, like Schnee's of Bozeman, Montana, that have created specialized combinations of features for elk hunting, including air bob soles, rubber bottoms, and tall leather tops, with or without insulation.

The bottom line, however, remains that you are going to face varying weather conditions and that just as you need various types and weights of clothing, you'll need various types of boots. For my own use, I wear a leather boot during the summer. During spring and fall, I wear a boot with a rubber bottom and leather top. For snowy conditions at the tail end of fall and during the winter, I wear an insulated boot. With these three types of boots, I make it through the year. And all of them have both good ankle support and some type of soft soles that allow me to walk quietly through elk country.

One other thing I should add about boots is that you'll get about what you pay for them. If there are items on your hunting equipment list that you should scrimp on, boots are not one of them. When you get those boots out in the mountains and put some miles on them, it won't take you long to learn whether you've chosen good ones or bad ones. Once you blister up or get footsore, you'll quickly learn that good footwear is at a premium in elk country.

Camouflage clothes are another matter. If we were hunting cattail marshes, camo wouldn't be a problem. If we were hunting oak forests back East, camo wouldn't be a problem. If we were sitting down, leaning with our backs against hardwoods, camo wouldn't be a problem. But I have yet to find a camouflage pattern that really suits a western elk hunter.

The problem out here in the West is that we have to blend in with the ground, more than we have to blend in with trees or leaves or cattails. That's where you're at 95 percent of the time, low to the ground, especially if you do a lot of calling. Depending on the part of elk country you hunt, you may also need to blend in with tan or yellow grasses, sagebrush, or pine forests.

I have yet to find the perfect western camo that covers all these things. Most camo patterns are too dark. Yet the lightest camo patterns are too light for use in pine forests. Like everything else in the clothing world, you have to compromise. Pick the camouflage pattern for the type of terrain you hunt the most. Or if your pocketbook can afford it, have two or three patterns and take your pick for where you plan to hunt.

In recent years, some new ideas on camouflage have emerged that will take some time to evaluate. The theories are interesting. But we'll have to wait and see if they pan out or not. There's one school of thought, for example, that is trying to analyze the color capabilities of animals' eyes. Their finding is that big game animals, like elk, can't distinguish the color blue from green. As a result, they're making blue camouflage clothing that will allow hunters to see each other easily, but will still apparently hide them from animals' eyes.

Another relatively new camouflage application for hunting is the ghilly suit, which has been used by the military and law enforcement for some time. These suits are custom

Chapter Six

ELK TACTICS

One of the best forms of camouflage is not moving, or waiting until an elk is looking in another direction before you move.

made of strips of cloth of various colors, sewn to the outside of a main liner of a coat. These strips of cloth add a three-dimensional look to the suit and, by the time you add a hood and gloves, offer complete concealment. The problem with them is that they are pretty much custom made, and you still might need several different suits for the types of terrain you plan to hunt. There's also the question of how a hunter might move through the brush or through tight timber in a suit that has all those strips of cloth hanging from it.

Until something better comes along, my personal preference for camouflage is a light cotton suit similar to cheese cloth that I can pull on over my other clothing. That works out best for me. If I'm out hunting and it's a very cold day, I can put on a coat underneath it. If I want to wear wool pants, the camo pants will fit over them. This type of camo doesn't add any warmth, just camouflages the clothing you wear underneath.

The downside of this camo is that it does wear out. It's thin, and it does tear. It does get caught on barbed wire fences and thorns. But it has worked out best for me.

While we're on the topic of camouflage, one thing we haven't covered is that the best camouflage of all is a person who is not moving, no matter what he or she happens to be wearing. Movement is the single, most critical part of not being detected by wildlife. If you are moving, it doesn't make any difference what you're wearing—the animal will see you. In the same vein, keeping a low profile will go a long way toward hiding you from animals' eyes. It has always amazed me, in fact, that when you hear stories from other hunters of how close animals came to them, it was never because the hunter was wearing the best camo. It was a matter of holding absolutely still, or lying down, or playing the wind right, or a combination of all these things.

I was filming a fellow once who had an elk tag while I was just filming. As the elk came in, you could tell just by the way the hunter acted that he had been around animals and had had them in close often. The first thing he did was to lie down flat on the ground. Filming, I got down as low to the ground as I could, too. As a result, the cow came right in.

Chapter Six

ELK TACTICS

She talked all the way in. She never suspected anything wrong because, by our profile, we didn't look like a threat. Had we remained upright, I can't say the same thing would have happened.

Does this mean we should abandon camouflage entirely or discount it completely? No. I'll use anything that helps hide me, just as I'll try to break up my outline with a tree, a rock, or a handy sagebrush. Just as I'll wear as quiet and warm a piece of clothing as I can. Just as I wear those quiet-soled boots.

Decoys

I really wish I could give you my clear-cut decision on using decoys for elk hunting. In truth, I have mixed feelings about them.

The notion of using something for the elk to look at, when you've called them in, has been around for a long, long time. It seemed only logical that an elk, coming in looking for another elk, would be easier to pull in close if there was something to look at besides the hunter.

With that in mind, my first attempt at decoying was to use a patch of elk hair. I tried it. It didn't work. It was more of a bother than it was worth. And it didn't seem like it helped my calling in elk, either. It was just something more to carry.

My first experiences with a deer decoy weren't exactly a raving success either. Now I know some guys have had success with them, especially on whitetails. The video footage I've seen of it is truly spectacular, of one whitetail buck charging and hooking the decoy with its antlers. But when I used a doe decoy on mule deer, it wasn't like that. We set a doe out in an alfalfa field and had her in a position where she looked like she was lying down. The other mule deer would just look at her and not pay much attention.

When Mel Dutton came out with an antelope decoy, I gave that a try, too. Here, I found success. Dutton's decoys were two-dimensional. You sort of folded them out to make a side view of a small buck antelope. I even gussied up my

Country that is open enough for an elk to see your decoy from a distance away is a real plus.

antelope decoy by putting in glass eyes, making the antelope look even more realistic.

With that antelope decoy, especially when we used it in conjunction with an antelope call, we got action. We could reel in bucks from long distances. It was exciting hunting. And it was fun.

Which brings us back to elk. Elk decoys have become more and more popular as a selling item in recent years. One of the first was a photographic image of a cow elk, a side view which was very realistic, but rather large.

Then Dutton came out with a more compact version, using the same principles he used on the antelope decoy. This decoy also folded out. It was a view of the rump of a cow elk, with the head looking back at you over the rump. It was smaller than the full side view and had the advantage of the decoy actually looking at you.

The first time we tried it, the elk knew we were there. We were clear back into the backcountry. We were going in for two weeks and figured we'd take the decoy along. We spotted a spike on a hillside. And even though he knew we were there, we set up the decoy and moved it out in front of us. When we started cow calling, the spike got real interested and started coming down, but never came in close. Of course, he had seen us, so that may have affected things.

Chapter Six

ELK TACTICS

On that trip, we tried the decoy a couple of other times in the timber and didn't have much luck. Without positive results to spur us to use it more, we didn't use it much. It was just one more thing to carry. We were hunting timber, where the field of view was limited. It didn't seem to be that good of an addition to the other equipment we already had to pack when we were hunting.

But this year, we got into a situation where we were hunting in more open country. The situation was a little more conducive to using a decoy. We decided to give it another try.

One thing we'd learned by this point was that the setup had to be just right for a decoy to work very well. You had to have some visibility. You needed some elk in the country to see the decoy, too. That opportunity presented itself one evening when we had a couple of bulls answer us in a relatively open drainage. We could even see one of the bulls, about eight hundred or nine hundred yards away.

My son Ryan, Murphy Love, and I were down on the creek bottom, and the bulls were above us. It was all open, except for a few trees between us and the visible bull. We didn't know where the other bull was, except that he was up that drainage and we could hear him. We set up the decoy far enough out in the open so the elk, if he got into a position five hundred or six hundred yards away, could see it.

We set up in a position where Ryan would be out in front, near the decoy, Murphy and I would be back a distance. It was the classic caller-and-shooter setup, except for the addition of the decoy. When the decoy was in place, we started bugling and cow-calling.

Working to our advantage was the time of day and the fact the bulls were getting more active. They answered the calls immediately, and we could see that the one bull was working in closer. We identified that bull as a six-point. We could hear the other bull coming closer, too. That one turned out to be a seven-point. Both were very respectable bulls.

When the six-point spotted the decoy, he came right in to seventy yards and stopped. From there, he studied the decoy, but couldn't seem to figure it out. The seven-point was a little farther back. When he came in and saw the six-point looking at this cow elk, he got all excited. He ran past that six-point like there was a race on. He ran right straight up to the decoy.

Ryan was lying just ten feet from the decoy and had just a little bit of brush in front of him. He was lying down flat on the ground. The seven-point bull finally came to a stop fifteen yards from the decoy. Ryan was making some real soft cow sounds. He'd do one. The elk's ears would perk up. It was obvious from the way the bull was acting that he hadn't come in to fight. He had something else on his mind.

Ryan had been spraying elk scent all the while the bull was coming in, and we could see the seven-point working his nostrils and licking his nose. But he seemed a little reluctant to come right in close. Instead, he started circling. That worked fine, until he got even with the decoy. At that point, all he could see was the thin edge—the cow he had been looking at had disappeared. This seemed to confuse him. He went from a high level of curiosity to a high level of tension, as it began dawning on him that something was wrong. The next time Ryan cow-called, the seven-point bolted. He jumped so hard and so fast that I thought he might have jumped on Ryan. Instead, he had jumped over the bank of the creek and on past it.

When the bull stopped on the other side, I cow-called to him. That held him, but he seemed to lose interest in Ryan's calls and started to be more interested in mine. That's when the six-point bull came in. This bull came in to within twenty yards of the decoy, but he was a bit cagier. He stayed at twenty yards. He didn't circle. He never came any closer and eventually went back the way he'd come in.

The whole little drama lasted about forty-five minutes, from start to finish, and even then, the bulls didn't leave. They moved off a distance and continued bugling until it got so dark that I couldn't shoot film any longer. In the darkness, they continued to bugle back and forth to each other.

In the end, I was amazed by how fast the animals came in to the decoy. I wondered whether or not having two bulls there had accelerated the action, with one bull trying to get

Chapter Six

■ *ELK TACTICS*

When you get a bull interested, sometimes he'll come in to an elk decoy very quickly.

to the cow ahead of the other.

In the process, I should also tell you that all the commotion attracted two cows, as well in the final waning moments of light. They also came running up to the decoy, but by then it was too dark to shoot any film. By that time, we were also using cow calls almost exclusively. The two cows answered these calls all the way in.

I'm left with mixed feelings about elk decoys and view

them as yet another piece of the elk hunting puzzle that we haven't quite put together yet. If a person had more time and more good setups, using decoys could be very interesting. I've talked to others who feel the same way.

I have talked to a hunter from Missoula, Montana, who has made a latex decoy and has shot a bull over it. He has called in other bulls, too.

I've heard of a person who has made an elk decoy out of fabric and uses cords to tie it off to nearby trees to stretch it out into position.

But based on my experiences so far, I'm giving decoys mixed reviews. I've had success with them. I've had my share of failures, too.

What I can tell you is that it takes a bit of extra effort to pack a decoy along with you. Some of them are bulky and cumbersome. Some of them make a lot of noise, both in packing them and in setting them up. Decoys for elk are not something you just toss in a pocket and bring along on the hunt.

But I'll also be honest with you and tell you that I'm not a master at decoying big game animals by any means. Maybe with time, I will be. As a result, as far as I'm concerned, the verdict is still out on elk decoys. Until we learn more, I'm not so sure that you couldn't accomplish the same goals with elk through calling correctly, using scent, and relying on your hunting skills for the rest.

Technology

Technology is a hot topic these days in the world of hunting. Perhaps it has always been. I can see it all now. The first time a caveman used a sharpened stick, instead of a blunt one, to stab a dinosaur, there was probably some other caveman who told him he was being unfair and ought to get back to more traditional weapons.

And so it is today. Hunters talk about the role of technology in their hunting. They argue about ethics. They wonder whether it's fair or unfair to use the latest gadgets and gizmos in their pursuit of wild game.

ELK TACTICS

In the process, some hunters also handicap themselves on purpose. Rather than hunt with a scoped modern rifle with the latest of loads, they go the way of black powder and use a percussion cap gun. Some guys think that's too modern and go with a flintlock. In archery, there are those who truly despise the cables and pulleys of compound bows and choose instead a more traditional recurve. And some think that's too modern and go with a longbow.

To me, all of these decisions are a matter of personal preference. The weapon you use is your choice, within the legal limits of the hunting regulations in the state where you happen to hunt. And those kinds of technological issues are more fit for the ethics books than they are for a book on hunting tactics.

There are some other technological tools that we will cover, however, because they get more to the core of tactics and are applicable no matter which weapon you happen to choose.

Among those tools are GPS units and altimeters and, lumping them together, person-to-person communications.

GPS (Global Positioning System) units are just starting to be used in outdoor applications, but they are already proving to be useful tools for hunters. While they won't actually find an elk for you, they can be most helpful in helping you locate yourself.

These units use satellites to help you pinpoint your latitude and longitude. They have memory to mark waypoints. They can help you retrace the steps you made or plot your steps in the future.

Ralph Saunders, a mapmaker and friend, has been using GPS units in elk country in all seasons. While he wouldn't throw away his map and compass in favor of GPS, he sees these units as another tool at a hunter's disposal.

For example, he was hiking during the summer when he located an elk wallow and a good rub area nearby. He marked the spot on his GPS unit so he would remember it and know how to get back to it during hunting season.

Another time, he was out in a vehicle on one of those big ranches, being shown around by somebody else, going

Hand-held GPS units can help hunters in a number of ways, including locating elk you knocked down back in the timber.

through gates, crossing pastures, seeing plenty of country. So he could find his way around the next time, he used the GPS unit to mark locations along the way.

Although he never used GPS to help locate a downed elk, he speculated that it would be a most valuable tool if you knocked down an elk at dusk, had to leave it there overnight, and then planned to return the following day to pack it out. In the past, guys would flag a trail out to mark the way, then follow the flags back in the next morning. With a GPS unit, all you'd have to know is the exact latitude and longitude of the downed animal to be able to return to the spot.

In terms of accuracy, Saunders said you're guaranteed to be within 100 meters of the spot where the elk would be. Most often, you're within 100 to 200 feet. In all but the densest timber, that's close enough for you to find a downed elk.

In most instances, he added, even the cheapest hand-held GPS units would be of value to a hunter. The more you pay for a unit, the more applications you have at your disposal.

Saunders said an altimeter is another useful tool in elk country that you can use along with your maps and compass. Altimeters read elevation and help you navigate your way through the mountains by helping to pinpoint your map position. If you know the elevation of a distant saddle you hope to reach, you can avoid unwanted radical climbs or going too far down the slope in your path to reach them.

Carl Wolf, another friend, said he also found altimeters to be useful in helping to find places where elk were likely to be. When he found the elevation zone that the elk were using, he'd take note of that elevation on an altimeter. Wolf found that when he worked similar elevation zones on other parts of the mountain, or in other parts of the mountain range, he would locate elk there, too. By making use of an altimeter, he eliminated a lot of country where the elk weren't likely to be.

Person-to-person communication devices are a bit more controversial. By person-to-person devices, I'm talking about two-way radios or cellular telephones.

In Montana, regulations have been passed against using two-way communications to help hunters in their pursuit of game. It isn't ethical, the state said, for hunters to close in on game, or direct other hunters to game, by the use of radios.

There are plenty of other stories, however, where two-way communications have been used to keep track of young hunters, or older hunters, to make elk hunting safer for them. There are stories of two-way radios saving hunters' lives, as well.

The talk on cellular phones is much the same. Some of the more perverse stories about cell phones involve hunters who actually use them to keep track of work, phoning back to the office, when they're elk hunting. That's really sick! There are other tales of people calling for rescues unnecessarily when they weren't really in danger, just inconvenienced by tough weather or tough going.

But there are rescue stories, too, of hikers and hunters who saved partners by being able to call for help in the quickest manner.

How much technology you choose to pack into elk country with you is a matter of personal choice. Some things help. Some aren't necessary. Some—like that cell phone to call work—are a plain nuisance.

Some hunters have abused two-way communications, using them to direct other hunters to herds of traveling elk.

Just remember that each piece of technology you bring along is one more thing you have to carry, and even if you're carrying it, it won't replace hunting skills in getting you an elk.

CHAPTER SEVEN

Troubleshooting

We do get letters. Sometimes lots and lots of letters. Some letters tell us about hunting success. For those hunters, it's a good feeling for them, and for us, too, to be able to celebrate their victories. Other letters tell about hunting troubles and problems. For those hunters, as much as possible, we try to help solve their dilemmas. In a way, those troubling letters are one of the bigger reasons why this book came about. In sharing those hunters' problems, and in sharing possible solutions, we're all able to learn a bit more about elk and elk hunting. It's that give-and-take about field experiences with elk that can make you—and me—better hunters.

I should tell you that, of all the letters I've received over the years, there are three of them that really stick in my mind, all for different reasons.

First off, there's a letter I received a while back from a guy from Iowa. He told me he was a big-time elk hunter. Then he went on to say he was completely disgusted with

ELK TACTICS

one of our books, *Elk Talk* or *The Elk Hunter*. He had nothing but bad things to say about it. We didn't know anything about elk. We didn't know anything about elk hunting. We were copying from other guys. We were passing out bad information. This Iowa guy knew elk. I guess we must have had a lot to learn from him.

Then, there was another letter from Jack Atcheson, of Butte, Montana. Jack is a Montana boy who has created a world-wide business over the years as a hunting consultant, and he has an international reputation as a hunter as well. But his roots are firmly in Montana, and his first loves are chasing elk and mule deer in the high country of home. Jack also read the books and sent a most complimentary letter about how good the books were. The books were so good, in fact, and we were so knowledgeable about elk, that Jack said if he found out he was hunting the same mountain we were, he'd move on because he knew the elk there were covered.

As to the guy from Iowa, it never ceases to amaze me how a guy who visits elk country for a week or two, even if he does it every year, thinks he knows everything about elk. He thinks he knows more than people who have lived in and around elk all their lives. As to Jack, that's high praise—in truth, too high praise. We don't have all the answers—perhaps not even as many as Jack has himself. But in placing our knowledge level and our personal successes somewhere between the statement of the guy from Iowa and the letter from Jack, we probably come closer to the truth.

For all of us, our knowledge of elk is still a work in progress. Some hunters know more. Some know less. If we only realize we don't know it all, then we're forced to pay attention and continue our lessons in the hope of learning more. And as we all learn, we grow.

As to that third memorable letter, I'll tell you about that later.

What I'd like to do in this chapter is answer some of the more common questions I've received in letters over the years and share some of the wisdom found in letters, too. Some of the recurring problems have been covered in depth

*A good rule of thumb for what bull sound to make:
Imitate the bull that's bugling to you.*

in other parts of this book, so bear with me if some answers sound hauntingly familiar. But in a question-and-answer format, maybe a new angle will be opened up for you and some new light will be shed on problems you've faced yourself.

Here are some of the questions readers have asked:

What kind of sounds should I make to a bugling bull?

As a general rule of thumb, I've always found my best success when trying to imitate the sound that a bull is making to me. But there are some qualifications to that state-

Chapter Seven

ment. On most occasions, when I'm first trying to get a bull to answer me, I use high-pitched sounds and shorter sounds. If I get a good response from that bull to the high-pitched, short sound and he's coming in, I'll keep using it. If it's working, why change? But if he's not coming in, and is responding only infrequently to the high-pitched sounds, I'll go almost immediately to imitating the sounds he's making.

How important are the grunts at the end of a bugle?

When I've judged elk-calling competition, it's obvious that a lot of callers think the squeals and grunts at the end of the call are very important. Those squeals and grunts go on and on—and sometimes on and on some more. In hunting situations, I'd say the squeals and grunts are only minimally important. Most real elk put two or three clean grunts at the end of their calls. Then they run out of air. The efficiency of modern elk calls makes it possible for hunters to not just imitate the sounds of an elk, but to make calls that are even better than those made by the elk themselves. That includes both the length of the high-pitched bugle and the length of the grunts at the end. For hunters who want to fine-tune their efforts to match real elk, the best thing you can do is to get a good audio cassette tape and imitate the actual sounds the elk are making on it. But please, keep peace in your family and do it in the car on the way to and from work. Too much bugling at home (that means anything over five minutes) is likely to drive your spouse crazy.

Can you tell the size of an elk by its bugle?

Judging the size of a bull by the bugle he makes is a very inexact science—but all hunters, including me, do it all the time. We hear this impressive bugle, and in our hearts, we know that it's got to be this huge bull. We hear a squeaky, high-pitched sound, and in our hearts, we know it's just a spike. The problem, in our hearts, is that often we're wrong. I've always felt that elk speak pretty much a common language. The sound we call calf calls, or cow calls, can be made by bulls, too, though often at just a shade lower pitch.

Elk country is huge, but you'll find there are some parts of it more likely to hold elk than others.

The same is true of bugles. From spikes through regal herd bulls, the calling sequence is basically the same. Those regal herd bulls may be a bit stronger, a bit more raspy, but the sequence is there. Problems come in when we try to cut hairs. If a big, old bull has been calling steadily day after day, I'm convinced that his throat gets sore. He gets called out. His voice turns raspy and hoarse, and his beautiful high notes turn into squeaks—about like what we call spike sounds. If a big bull is calling from his bed, unable to pump himself up and move his body freely as he does when he's on his feet, the sound is affected, too. When you get down to the differences in sound between a spindly raghorn and a respectable six-point satellite bull, the distinction can again be difficult. So while we all, in our hearts, paint a mental picture of the bulls we hear, the truth of the matter is that often those pictures aren't as accurate as we might like them to be.

How do I make deep, raspy sounds with a bugle?

To start with, it has always been my feeling that what guys call deep, raspy sounds are the normal bugling sequence of a bull whose voice is bugled out. Think about it, as the rut progresses, action around those harems gets more and more frequent. It isn't just a morning-evening affair, but all times of the day and night. When a bull answers back to every bugle within earshot, eventually he gets bugled out. His voice gets deeper. It gets raspier. It's about like a human coming down with laryngitis. Hunters who like to imitate the sounds they're hearing from a bull have sought to imitate that deep, raspy sound. That usually requires manipulating your call with your voice. You throw your own voice sound into the sound that the call is making. You go something like "uh, uh, uh" into the call. The end result of the combination of your voice and the call is similar to the deep, raspy sounds a bugled-out bull makes. But it takes some practice in the off-season to do it well. If you practice, you can do it with about any type of bull call. The call I manufacture, sell, and use, the "Power Bugle," has an external rubber band that makes making a raspy sound a little easier than with some other calls. You put your lips directly on the top of the band, pucker your lips like you're going to blow a trumpet, and let your lips vibrate like they do on a horn as you blow. If you do that against the band, it makes a deep, raspy sound.

Every time I go out, I get into lone cows. How do I get into bulls?

If you're getting into lone cows, don't change a thing. It's just a matter of time before that elk coming in is wearing some headgear. What a person wants to remember is that, when they get into a lone-cow situation, often they're cows on the tail end of a herd or on the side of a herd. During the rut, elk are generally in groups. Some groups may be small. Others can be large. But bulls rarely allow a loose cow to go unattended at that time of year. It's far more likely to run into a lone bull than a lone cow or calf. So if you do call in a cow, that's the time to be most vigilant in scanning the timber nearby. In truth, about the only time in fall that I've run into lone cows is when the animal has been injured. It might have a hurt leg, be sick, or be suffering some other malady. Sometimes, elk will go off by themselves until they heal up. But healthy cows just about always have a healthy bull somewhere nearby.

How do you improve your success with bulls?

This has been a common question as sort of a spin-off of the previous one. The answer is pretty much the same. You improve your success with bulls by trying to keep tabs on the cows. If you can keep tabs on the cows, the bulls will come. The only disclaimer I'd like to add to this contention is for elk populations that are completely out of whack. If bulls have been overshot in your area, perhaps you have bull-cow ratios that are extremely poor. If that's the case, you need to look for a new area to hunt. Just as you can't take trophy bulls from an area that has no trophies, your odds of taking any bull are poor if the bull-cow ratio is too low. Move on. Pioneer a new hunting area.

What types of calls should I use if I'm a beginner?

Good advice for a beginner is good advice for me to remember, too. Keep your calls simple. Keep your calls short. Keep your calls not too loud. In three words, keep your calls simple, short, sweet. Many times, callers will have a tendency to blow their calls too loud. They'll also make them more complicated than they really need to be. Short bull sounds. Short cow sounds. Both are very effective. And if you call too loudly, and the elk are too close, you could blow the elk out in front of you, instead of arousing their curiosity and bringing them in for a close look.

Do elk calls work in all seasons?

Cow and calf sounds most definitely work in all seasons. Bull sounds work pretty much only in the months and weeks before, during, and just after the rut. Cow and calf sounds work well all through the remainder of the hunting season and even into the late seasons we have here in Montana—special permit hunts that run clear into February. In fact, I've found that cow and calf sounds sometimes work better and better as it gets later in the year. Elk under

Chapter Seven

ELK TACTICS

After the peak of the rut, cow calls will remain very effective in calling in bulls, while bugling will become less and less effective.

stress—whether they're stressed by the prospect of being fatally wounded by an arrow or stressed by harsh winter conditions—sometimes respond the best of all. Why? I can't tell you. But I know I've stopped elk that were running away with an arrow in them, had them stand there and bleed out on the spot. And I've stopped and held elk on the winter range for long periods of time while hunters have gotten into position to take a standing shot at them. If you learn to make the basic sounds, even a beginner can enjoy success with a call.

Why don't rubber bands in calls hold up better?

Most rubber used in elk calls is latex rubber. That's true whether you're using a rubber band bite-and-blow call like "Cow Talk" or the "Power Bugle" or the thin sheets of an inside-the-mouth diaphragm call. It's a matter of trying to use the material that makes the best elk sounds. But latex is not the most durable of materials. It's especially sensitive to sunlight. It dries and cracks with age, too. And anyone who has simply thrown one in a pocket, then stuck it to their lips or in their mouth without looking, can attest to the fact that they're real magnets for dust and dirt. All of these things take a toll on latex. As long as latex continues to make the best sound, however, you're going to have to work around it. For rubber band-type calls, that means carrying an extra band or two along. For diaphragm calls, it means packing an extra call or two. If you're looking to extend the life of a call, all I can tell you is to take extra good care of them. Put them in a pouch, plastic bag, or container when you're not using them. Keep them out of the sunlight when you store them. And try to keep them free of dust and dirt.

Elk country is so huge. Where do you start?

Elk country is huge. Mountain ranges may run for fifty or one hundred miles. There are countless creek drainages, peaks, and trails. That's certainly enough to intimidate any newcomer. As a result, there's a premium on doing your homework before hunting season arrives. If you're looking for an area to hunt, talk to people—a lot of people. Public land agencies are often good places to start with maps and personnel familiar with wildlife. Then move on to area sportsmen's groups, sporting goods stores, or local hunters. Try to figure out which of the drainages are more productive than others. Learn about access to the area. Remember that you need some access to get in there in the first place, but too much access may mean the area is hunted too hard to hold many elk or many big bulls. Choose your hunting area carefully. In the hunting equation, choosing the right spot to look for elk will be far more critical to your hunting success than what bow you shoot, what caliber rifle you use, or even how good you are with an elk call.

Must I visit an area before I go hunting there?

This question is both easy to answer, and very, very tough. On the one hand, I can tell you truthfully that there's no substitute for visiting an area prior to the elk hunting season, so you can physically walk the area, check it out, and see what's there. On the other hand, if you're coming from another state or from far across the same state, the decision to do this is not easy, or cheap. If you can visit the area before the season, start by checking out the elk you see to determine if they are the size and type you're looking for. But beyond that, look for the telltale signs that will tip you off to elk use in the season you plan to be there. These signs might be rubs on trees. They might be wallows. They could be trail networks in marshy areas of high basins. Any and all of those things could tip you off to a good place to make bull and cow sounds during the rut. Signs of old elk use, and seeing elk anywhere in the area, may mean that your quest in hunting season comes down to figuring out the exact elevation where the animals are holding and then keying in on it. Pre-season scouting will have provided you with a pretty good idea of where the elk will be. If you're from out-of-state and can't make it there for pre-season scouting, you can rely on an outfitter who will have that pre-season knowledge for you. Or, if you talk to enough people, you might be able to figure it out for yourself—but that's a pretty big "might."

What tactics are successful with reluctant bulls after the peak of the rut?

While bull sounds are highly effective during the rut, their effectiveness tapers off the longer it goes beyond the peak of the rut. Some bulls may still be bugling. But their urge to come in to another bugle isn't nearly as strong. My tactics at that time of year tend more toward the cow call and use of elk urine as a cover scent. With a combination of the two, archery hunters can still lure in bulls until the tail end of October. In my part of the elk hunting world, in fact, cows that weren't bred the first time around will come back into heat in late October. When that happens, you might catch a late bull interested in coming in to bull sounds. But, for the most part, it's a cow call and elk scent season by that time of the year.

Should we pressure passive bulls or be more patient?

That's a toughie. And I'm not sure there's one answer that would fit all situations, either. There are really two schools of thought on this. One school is to keep pushing the bull and if you only push him long enough and hard enough, he'll eventually turn around and come back to you. That does work, but you've got to keep after him, and after him, and after him. Not all mountain conditions allow you to do that. The other school of thought is to be patient. Work the bull more gently with cow sounds. Try not to move the bull out of the area, but keep working him with the sounds. Over a period of time, the bull's curiosity will finally be aroused, and he, or another bull, will come over to investigate. In a long-calling situation like this one, scent can also be helpful. The longer you stick in one spot, the more likely it is that a swirl of wind will give you away.

How important is calling compared to other hunting skills?

Calling is just one hunting skill. It cannot stand alone. You have to add other hunting skills to it to become a complete elk hunter. And, increasingly, it is the elk hunters who are most complete who are consistently finding success. Once

ELK TACTICS

Elk are adept at handling natural barriers including swift-moving rivers and lakes.

an elk smells you, the game is pretty much over. Once an elk sees you, he isn't likely to come close enough for a shot. Once an elk hears calls that aren't like those made by real elk, or hears unnatural sounds in his mountains, the hunt is pretty much ruined. In the old days, when elk weren't pressured so much, hunters could get by with fewer skills. The elk would tolerate a few mistakes, too. Today, even the most skilled hunters can run into difficulties. Calling isn't a cure-all. It's just one of the weapons that a hunter has in his arsenal. It's an effective weapon. But it most assuredly cannot stand alone.

How do I pick an outfitter?

If I could sum it up in a few words, I would say, "word of mouth." That remains one of the best ways to make sure you have a good and reputable outfitter to take you into elk country. You can hear about outfitters many ways. Outfitters are found at most sports and outdoor shows. You can look them up on the Internet. You can read their ads in the back pages of magazines. But to simply choose one that way, put down a big down payment, then arrive in elk country and hope for the best is an extremely risky way to go. Most good and reputable outfitters have built their businesses on return customers. If an outfitter doesn't have many, there has to be a reason for it. When you talk to an outfitter, ask for a list of his former clients and make sure it's a long list. Then call a bunch of them. Don't be shy. Ask about the outfitter's camp or lodging arrangements, including the beds. Ask about the meals. What exactly did the outfitter serve for breakfast and dinner, and what was the lunch you packed along for the middle of the day? Ask about the pack stock, if it's to be a trip into the backcountry. Ask about vehicles or if you'll be packing that elk out on your back. Ask about hunting success, and be specific with your questions. Set your goals for yourself and then choose an outfitter to meet those goals. Do you want a cow, a raghorn bull, a trophy bull, or the first thing that comes along? And don't be embarrassed by either asking about it, or the goals you set. For a lot of hunters, any elk at all is enough to satisfy the dream of an elk hunt. And given the choice, I'd just as soon have a winter's worth of steaks from a fat cow as an old bull. But, if you want a big bull, make sure that the outfitter is hunting an area that can provide it and that he has the track record of providing them for other hunters. Ask about how many hunters there are per guide. In short, talk, talk, talk, and make sure you trust the person who's giving the answers. A good outfitted hunt is worth every penny you pay for it and a hefty tip at the end of the trip, too. A bad outfitted hunt isn't worth a dime.

How do I find my own Amazon?

Well, as I said at the beginning of this chapter, we've received three really memorable letters over the years. The third one had to do with the search for an Amazon, some warrior woman of the wilderness.

The letter came from some guy who was back in the bush in British Columbia who had just read our first two elk books and had become inspired by them. He was writing to say that they had fired him up completely to try his

ELK TACTICS

luck at bowhunting for elk the following fall.

The guy said he was forty-five years old, had hunted for thirty-five of those years, and was taught his skills by old prospectors and trappers. The sounds of a bugling bull elk were music to his ears, and the notion of calling them in close and taking them with an arrow was an inspiration.

But then he went on about his personal life. "I'm on the track of a female," he wrote, "particularly a heavy frame one, who can pack out moose and elk, a real Amazon. Blue eyes, blond hair, soft discipline, Christian, 25 years old, with a good sense of humor and a backhoe. Any ideas?"

What could I say then? What can I say now?

I don't care how long you've been hunting—elk or Amazons—there are still some questions that are best left unanswered.

EPILOGUE

Down the Trail

I was hunting with my sons, and everything was just perfect. We were in a really good spot, near a recently used wallow. Fresh signs of elk were everywhere, all over the country. We had moved into the area quietly. And I had begun to call.

After a call or two, we sat there together listening, straining our ears for the sound of an elk calling back to us. No call came. But there were some sounds out there. As we listened, we could hear the footfalls of elk—not just one elk, but a number of them. They were moving through the timber below us, their hooves making wooden knocking sounds as they walked.

Calling blind requires listening for all those sounds, not just the bugles. That comes from experience and good hearing. As I have gotten older, I don't have the luxury of hearing all those sounds like I did when I was younger. That happens to all of us. But still, there are those sounds you listen for.

ELK TACTICS

What I could hear down in the timber was more than one elk as they went over some deadfall. The front part of their hooves hit the deadfall and made a knocking sound that carried quite well. I motioned to my ears and pointed down the hill. My sons heard and took note.

It was a bunch of elk moving through. We had them coming to us. We waited there for about an hour and made a couple of more cow sounds after that. But the elk weren't coming. They were not responding to our calls. They were simply moving through.

After about an hour, we slipped down into the timber after them. By reading the sign and looking at their tracks, we could see that they were going away from us. So we picked up their tracks and started following them. And we could see that they moved into a place nearby, which looked suspiciously like it would be their bedding area.

Had we been hunting that area for a number of days, we probably would have left the elk there. But this was a one-day hunt. If we bumped the elk and spooked them, so be it. We wouldn't be back the next day anyway. But if we moved very slowly and stalked them in there, perhaps we'd get close enough for a shot.

We did just that, moving slowly, using our binoculars to penetrate the dense timber ahead of us. We moved quietly. We were doing pretty well. In fact, we did too well. Our sneak resulted in a situation where we had moved right into the middle of the herd without knowing it. But, as you might imagine, once the elk knew it, they didn't like it one bit.

The forest suddenly exploded with the crashes of spooked elk. They were so close. They were so spooked. It sounded like the whole forest was going to crash in around us. It was incredibly exciting. And we didn't get an elk. We didn't even get a shot.

I mention this story, because the experience was so memorable. It is a memorable story despite the fact that there wasn't a tagged elk at the end of the trail.

When I think back on all the elk hunting experiences I've had, so many of them came about without a tagged elk at the

You don't have to tag an elk to come away from elk country with some spectacular memories.

end. There were close encounters with big bulls. There were stalks made and blown. There were times spent enjoying some beautiful country with family and friends. There were cows and calves and bulls of all ages that I've seen near and far and everywhere in between.

My successes in actually shooting elk are small in comparison. The same is true of people who portray themselves as experts. Some fractional amount of my total encounters with elk will result in one that ends up in my freezer. Sometimes that's because I'm out in the field filming, rather than hunting. Other times, it's because the elk I call in aren't the ones I want to shoot. Still other times—and I'm being honest with you—it's because I couldn't find an elk, didn't call one in, or made a mistake as I did with the elk in the story above.

All of these things are part of elk hunting—the successes and the failures. But amid it all is some spectacularly beautiful country. There are hunting camps, with good food and good fellowship. There are opportunities to spend more time with sons and daughters, fathers and grandfathers, wives, brothers, sisters, cousins, uncles, and aunts. These experiences are more difficult to get a handle on. How do you measure the beauty of a golden stand of aspens in fall? How do you rate the beauty of a snowfall as the big flakes float down through the pine trees? What is the value of sharing a good sitting log with someone you care about and resting your eyes with a view of distant mountain peaks?

Becoming a good elk caller is a skill you can be proud of. Becoming a veteran hunter, with all the skills to show for it, is an accomplishment that isn't earned overnight.

In a book like *Elk Tactics,* it's easy to tell the tales and describe the strategies you have to learn to become more efficient in filling your elk tag. That's nuts-and-bolts stuff that is easily passed along. But how do you impart a deep gut feeling for the elk themselves and the splendor of the country that these elk call home? How do you get it across that there are lessons to be learned about these things, too, and that we all need to fight to protect these wild places?

The ingredients for becoming a good elk hunter are relatively simple. You need to know where to look for the animal. You need to know its habitat and its patterns. You need to know how to make a good setup. You need to know how to make good sounds. You need to have patience. And you need to be prepared for elk, and elk tactics, to change over time.

In *Elk Talk,* the first book of this trilogy on elk hunting, we wrote: "There's a lot we don't know about how animals communicate. We are just starting to understand." The same thing could be said today. We know calling works. We know how to make good sounds. We're still discovering new things about calling. What works in one instance so well may not work in the next instance at all.

But none of that takes anything away from the hunting experience itself.

The joys of elk hunting are many. The joys of calling elk are many, as well. And putting a tag on an elk is certainly a noble goal. But my best tactic, and my fondest wish for you, is that you enjoy every bit of your time in elk country, cherish it, and tuck your experiences away in your heart, to live in your memory forever. If you only do that, you will be a successful elk hunter.

The joys of elk hunting are many, including just sharing the mountaintops with this spectacular animal.

Epilogue

Other books from E.L.K., Inc., by Don Laubach and Mark Henckel:

ELK TALK

Elk talk, the language, and *Elk Talk,* the book, together form the new revolution in the elk hunting world. Elk talk, the language, is a complete calling system of cow talk, calf talk, and bull talk that lures elk to within rifle, bow, or camera range. It works on all elk. It works in all seasons. And it works in every part of elk country.

THE ELK HUNTER

Great elk hunters are made, not born. Through the course of their lives, they pick up pieces of the elk-hunting puzzle, putting them together until they discover the whole picture and become consistently successful at the game. *The Elk Hunter* takes you through a hunter's lifetime in a personal way, finding the pieces of the elk-hunting puzzle as a hunter would. You'll learn about hunters in the old days and how they did it. You'll learn the state-of-the-art methods being used today.

DEER TALK

If you're dreaming of a big buck within hunting range or just a doe or fawn within range of your camera, *Deer Talk* will make your dream come true. The revolutionary system of communicating with mule deer and whitetails described in this book has produced some startling results wherever it's been tried. It lures deer out of their beds and out of heavy cover. It stops them in their tracks when they're running away. It calms them when they're nervous. And, best of all, it works in all seasons.

These books can be ordered from E.L.K., Inc., by calling: 1-800-272-4355.